W9-CHS-853

MONEY TALKS

IT SAYS GOOD-BY

MONEY TALKS

IT SAYS GOOD-BY

by Bill King

with Pat King

WOMEN'S AGLOW FELLOWSHIP
Lynnwood, WA 98036

© Copyright 1977 by Women's Aglow Fellowship

Lynnwood, WA

All rights reserved

Printed in the United States of America

ISBN: 0-930756-31-2

Table of Contents

Introduction

THE MISSIONARY LOOKED SQUARELY at the congregation as he continued, "God will not be outdone in generosity. Any financial sacrifice you make for starving children in India will be returned to you, over and over."

My eyes met Pat's, then we both glanced at our young son sitting contentedly between us. Mentally contrasting his life with the children of the mission in India, I wondered what to do. I pulled out my wallet and gazed at the two five-dollar bills in it, knowing we needed every bit of that money to get through the coming month. Pat reached over, plucked one of those fives out and dropped it in the collection plate. I was so shocked, I nearly yelled at the usher to bring it back!

Walking home, we discussed our financial situation and speculated on how we would get by the rest of the month on five dollars. Having recently purchased our first real home, we hardly had any money. Moving costs and fall tuition for my night school had left us with ten dollars for food and bus fare. Now we had only five left. I had no idea how we would get by. That evening as Pat was preparing dinner, the elderly man whose garden ran alongside our house, appeared at the back door. "Here," he said, thrusting a box of squash and corn into my arms. "I thought you young people could use these."

Later that same evening another neighbor appeared at our door to inquire if we had a car.

"No," Pat smiled, "We're lucky to have a house."

The neighbor seemed delighted. Turning to me he asked, "I wonder if I could rent your garage?" He held out some money. "Does a dollar a week sound fair?" As I nodded I could see the sparkle in Pat's eyes. A dollar a week was exactly what I needed for bus fare.

The next day a woman with two children came up the walk.

7

The woman introduced herself as Mrs. Edwards and said she had seen us in church.

"I hate to ask you this when you don't know me," she went on, "but my husband needs me with him on a business trip. I have a sitter coming on week days, but could you possibly take care of our children for the next three weekends? I can pay you five dollars a weekend."

"God has really provided!" Pat announced as she told me the good news that evening.

"How do you know it wasn't just a coincidence?" I asked.

"Because of what she said."

"What?"

"That she had asked God to show her who would be a good person to watch her children. It was as if He directed her eyes right to us."

"So?"

"I asked her when she had asked God, and she told me it was right after the offering."

This incident, as much as anything I have learned during the years I have spent in my profession of budgeting and financial planning, has shaped my philosophy of life, which is reflected in this book. God is the giver, we know that. However, He expects us to do our share, too. This book provides a look at the cooperative adventure of our God who gives, and Christians who choose to be stewards of His gifts.

Before I begin writing about money, there is one Scripture verse I'd like to discuss: Matthew 6:33. Jesus had climbed to the top of the hill and was sharing with the housewives, the craftsmen, and the fishermen who crowded around Him. He told them of God's great love and concern. He told them not to worry about *things*, such as food, drink, or clothes. He talked about the heavenly Father's care for the birds and the flowers. Then He said something of the utmost importance:

> Your heavenly Father will give you all that
> you need if you will give Him first place in your
> life and live as He wants you to.

> Matthew 6:33, The Living Bible

If you will give Him first place in your life. Without these ten words the contents of this book become merely another of

8

many "how to" manuals. However, when you take them seriously and make Jesus first in your life, then everything you read and make an effort to apply to your situation will have a strength beyond your own understanding. If asking Jesus to be in first place is a commitment you made many years ago, but have not kept current, take time right now to recommit your life to Him.

This book is filled with choices you can make to bring you to new freedom in money matters. The most important choice has already been made, if Jesus is first in your life.

Pat and I have already prayed for God's blessings in the lives of all the readers of this book. We know that with His help you are going to find enough money to live the abundant life He has in store for you.

Bill King
Summer, 1977

1
Two Who Chose

A WELL-KNOWN CHRISTIAN LEADER recently declared, "Using charge accounts is wrong for Christians. I have burned every charge-plate I have ever owned." He went on to quote the verse from the Bible, "Owe no man anything." To him this meant that using charge accounts is not in God's will.

I don't know what effect his statements had on the people under his leadership, but I suspect they caused a certain amount of frustration. The families who lived by credit probably didn't know what to do. Those who had a half-cash, half-charge life style may have agreed with him and followed his example. Those of us who knew this man's present financial status only chuckled. We knew he had just received a windfall of over $5,000 which allowed him to clear up his accumulated small debts and begin afresh.

Most people don't receive surprise checks written in four figures. A pay check coming every week or two, or only once a month, is the total source of revenue for most families today. Payday-to-payday living is what gives charge accounts their impetus. A friend of mine who is a conservative banker was so embarrassed when his bank went into the charge card business, he apologized for them. Today he admits his colleagues had a vision that he hadn't shared. A large part of his bank's economy is financed by the incredible interest received from charge card customers.

We have become a nation built on credit. At one time only the wealthy had charge accounts. Now every wage earner is wooed relentlessly by merchants to come in, buy what he wants, and pay later. I grinned as I read a recent ad that proudly proclaimed, "Now the *Pay-As-You-Shop* store is accepting bank credit cards." I have heard that in some places you can even charge your charitable contributions!

With all the pressures on us to use credit, is it any wonder that Christian families are in debt as badly as the non-Christian Joneses next door? Credit purchasing is a way of life. It is a way that ruins marriages; a way that makes irresponsibility an easy course to follow; a way that destroys earning power. Yet, despite all that you may have heard about the evils of charging, despite the awful traps that credit poses, despite the financial jam you may be in right now because of your recent and not-too-recent charge purchases, *there is nothing wrong with having and using a charge account*. More about this later.

As you read this book you will learn how to handle your money. You will discover what a personal financial plan is, and how to set up your own plan to allow you to be debt-free. Your plan will take the mystery out of your money situation, letting you know what you can realistically spend on food and how much you should charge on your charge account. Once you know where you stand financially the choice you make of what to purchase and what not to purchase will bring God's blessing into your life.

Right now it might be that Satan has more control over your money than you do. He knows that if you overspend and your finances get totally out of control, your marriage will be weakened. If he can get you so far in debt that there seems no way out, he knows you will look to the hope of more money instead of hope in Jesus Christ for a solution. Satan tempts you, cajoles you, and persuades you to go against your conscience to buy one more thing. He wants to put your family in the deepest debt he can. One of the reasons it's so easy to listen to him is because most people really aren't sure where they should draw the line in their spending. Don't let a retail store's credit statement guide you. Statistics show that stores allow you to charge 250 percent more than you can ever pay back!

Once you have read this book and work a plan out for your situation, you will know how to choose what to buy and when to buy it. You will be free from Satan's temptations to buy too much, and that's where the blessing comes in. To understand this blessing, let's look at someone in the Bible who Satan tempted to acquire a few extra baubles for his family and himself.

The scene (recorded in chapter 7 of the Book of Joshua)

opens with the Israelites being beaten in battle. Then it shifts to Joshua lying on the ground crying out to the Lord because of the defeat. The Lord tells Joshua that someone among the Israelites has disobeyed and, contrary to orders, has taken some previously gathered loot into his own tent instead of destroying it as directed. Through a process of elimination, Joshua finally confronts Achan, who admits that he coveted a beautiful robe from Babylon as well as gold and silver. He has taken them home and hidden them. In the end, Achan and his entire family are stoned to death.

The present day analogy is obvious. Achan's family and property were destroyed because he chose to obtain something about which the Lord had said "no." Too often families are ruined and possessions scattered when covetousness leads to the purchases of things that the Lord doesn't feel are necessary.

On the other hand, we can take a look at someone in the Bible who chose differently, with good results. Joseph, sold into slavery in Egypt, rose to the position of overseer, with responsibility for everything the Egyptian leader, Potiphar, owned. Then Potiphar's wife made eyes at Joseph and suggested he come and sleep with her. Potiphar's wife could have been another possession for Joseph to acquire. Yet Joseph chose to be the good steward of Potiphar's goods that God expected him to be. He chose not to acquire something that God did not mean for him to have. The immediate result, the Bible tells us, was a prison term. The long-range results brought more wealth and prestige than Joseph had ever dreamed of. See the Book of Genesis, chapters 39-43.

A modern-day parallel is a man who chooses not to cross God's will by acquiring a certain item. Your charge accounts can allow you to be like Joseph. If you desire to be a faithful steward of all that God has given you, begin by working out your own financial plan and sticking to its guidelines.

At first the results may feel like the confines of prison. But be faithful. Ultimately, God will bless you and your family. Every time you say no to the temptation to charge what you *can't afford* and yes to God's prompting, you invite His blessing.

As this book teaches you how to set up your financial plan, it should change not only your financial picture, but your whole life.

2
How a Financial Plan Works

"BILL, WHAT ARE WE GOING TO DO?"

As we went over the church account books, the pastor's voice held a concerned note.

"Each year our costs go up but contributions stay about the same. This year we have to face some major repairs that will completely wipe out our savings."

The previous pastor had been a frugal man who hated to spend a cent on himself or the church. His coat was always good for one more winter and while the church was kept neat and clean, it was always, "We can wait until next year to repair the roof or the furnace." He was able to accumulate a small savings account and never had to call on his people for extra money.

Two years after he died, the new pastor was being forced into making some decisions. We were working on a financial plan to assist him in making the proper ones. Because he was doing God's work I felt that a spending plan was necessary. In this way he would know which expenditures *had* to be made, which ones should be made as additional contributions came in, and which were possible when the Lord sent the money for them. The plan would not put a limit on his activities but be a guide for the pastor.

A guide, or financial plan, is something all churches and other religious institutions should have. By realistically developing and following a plan, not only can right financial choices be made but a considerable amount of energy can be saved by not worrying over unknown problems.

Most people expect their pastors to know how much is being spent on salaries, upkeep, choir robes, organ repair, and all the other details of running a church. They would be shocked if their pastors professed to not knowing where the church money was being spent!

Yet, too often those same people have no plan for spending their own money. They have no idea of the cost of their clothing and household expenses. Often while I'm preparing an individual income tax return, my client will lament, "I don't know where all that money went. We haven't a thing to show for it."

If you are one of the people who isn't sure where your money is going but know it doesn't stretch far enough, then more than a raise, more than a second job, your greatest monetary need is for a personal financial plan.

Every family should have a plan for managing their financial resources. People with low or fixed incomes need to know what their basic cost of living is, so they can determine the amount of money they have to spend on other things. Every family, no matter how large or small its income is, needs a plan to keep money from slipping through their fingers.

Well-to-do persons need a financial plan as much as anyone else. Their greater buying power enables them to buy a greater number of unnecessary items than other people, although over-spending takes longer to catch up with them. It is amazing how many well-off people are caught in a financial bind and can't seem to find a way out.

When you started out managing your own money you probably had some kind of financial plan: perhaps an informal, unwritten one. As time passed and you gained financial responsibilities, it became more difficult to assess your financial picture. After you were married, money arguments possibly tended to appear. Sometimes you may have become dishonest with your spouse about your spending.

A written financial plan would have saved much of your trouble by allowing you to know your problem areas and finding the means of fixing them. It also would have stopped potential problems before they brought financial disaster.

One of the main reasons people do not develop personal financial plans is that they think they have to follow them exactly once they have been made. This is not true. A plan is a guide, a help, and a tool; it should not become an inflexible dictator. A plan is a guideline that can be constantly revised. For instance, if you allow $20 for a monthly phone bill in your plan and spend $25, you have not necessarily overspent. You have revised your plan.

Six months is usually a long enough period to cover with

your first financial plan. It can be redone and revised during this time. The more you work with it the more accurate and helpful it will be. Remember, *your financial plan is your servant*. It should be flexible enough so that if you overspend you can change the plan instead of having a confrontation with it!

A financial plan is not nearly as difficult as it sounds. When I was a boy in school I remember the teacher announcing that we would begin to learn about fractions. The class moaned outloud. We had all heard that fractions are hard. The teacher, sensing how we dreaded tackling something so difficult, put us at ease. "Why, what's the trouble? You've been using fractions since kindergarten."

"We have?"

"Haven't you ever divided an apple in quarters or cut a candy bar in half? Well, you were using fractions!"

I remember the relief that flooded through me as I realized I had already had some experience with what I thought was so hard to learn. You, too, have had some experience in financial planning. Whether it's a method of putting all the bills in one place and shuffling through them on payday to find the most critical ones; paying only late or second notices; or putting bills in an orderly sequence to pay on or before due dates, you have made a start with a financial plan.

If you are thinking, as you consider a financial plan, "Financial plans don't work" or, "We've tried it before" or, "I'm doing everything I can now but I still can"t make it," your feelings are only natural. But before you give up, read about Andrew and his wife and the personal financial plan that worked for them.

Andrew Carter was a full-time student at the University of Washington when we got together to discuss his financial situation and prepare a budget. Andrew had grown up in Kenya, Africa. He spoke excellent English, was studying engineering, and would return to his country to teach and practice it. His wife, Areba, was with him and in the three years they lived in the United States they had become quite Americanized. While examining their financial situation I found Andrew's income came from a quarterly stipend he received as a teaching assistant, a modest monthly scholarship from Kenya, and a weekly salary from a part-time job.

Looking over the Carters' expenses I saw they lived simply. They had typical expenses: rent, utilities, car and medical insurance, food, automotive, and personal (miscellaneous) expenses. In addition Andrew spent as much as possible on books, building a library to take back to Kenya. They had no charge accounts, but they did have a loan from the university credit union. This loan had been taken out to pay the uninsured part of a doctor and hospital bill resulting from the birth of their son about six months earlier. Andrew also used some of the loan to purchase books. Their only exorbitant expense was their phone bill. This was because Areba's sister, the only person she knew in this country who spoke her native dialect, lived on the East Coast. This sister was like an oasis to Areba when she was overwhelmed with loneliness.

After we determined where all their income was coming from and what their expenses were, we put together a six-month cash projection to see where the Carters were headed. We first took into consideration the number of paydays in each month. Since the six-month period included December we put in an estimate for Christmas expenses. When we completed the forecast, it showed that for four of the six months their expenses were more than their income. For the six-month period their total expenses were $275 greater than their income. This $275 was about what Andrew earned in one month. Areba looked discouraged and Andrew was embarrassed, although neither one was surprised.

Moving quickly to encourage Areba and overcome Andrew's embarrassment, we looked at each item of expense to see what could be done. Andrew felt nothing could be done since they were already being very cautious with their money. During our review, however, we found seven areas of savings that could reduce their expenditures and give them an additional $55. Areba couldn't believe they were not going to need to borrow more money. We all knew it would be hard and there would be setbacks, but Andrew also felt it would be worth making any changes necessary to get on a financially sound basis.

Here is a summary of the changes we decided on:
(1) Move to lower-rent apartment.
(2) Lower the heat during the nighttime. The Carters, from a much warmer climate, were keeping their apartment at the same level of heat twenty-four hours a day.
(3) Reduce the number of long distance phone calls. Areba agreed to call her sister only on specific days, and not

16

whenever she felt like it. She agreed to set the length of her conversation before she called and to try to call when the rates were lowest.

(4) Start to shop once a week for their groceries from a list and try to plan their menus around sale items.

(5) Consider carefully the purchase of every miscellaneous item, putting it off as long as possible.

(6) Bake or make as many Christmas gifts as possible.

(7) Pay car insurance semi-annually and save the monthly service charge.

(8) Hold off purchasing additional books, other than required text books for six months.

On the next four pages are copies of the actual schedule used to help Andrew and Areba. As you look at them keep in mind the fact that they were worked up before our present inflationary situation.

After listing their total income and expenses on the first schedule, we made a six-month cash projection. This showed that at the end of the six months they would be $275 behind. By making necessary changes they could end up $33 ahead.

Neither their projection or budget have any allowance for contributions to church or charity. I discussed this with Andrew but the omission didn't bother him.

The Carters attempted the changes I suggested. They were successful in reducing their costs, although Areba periodically made too many long-distance phone calls and Andrew did not completely stop buying books. At the end of six months, however, they were ready to try another six-month budget. The most important effect of their first budget was that they did not have to borrow any money.

In later chapters we will discuss your own financial plan, but Andrew and his situation can acquaint you with the basic tool of financial planning: the four schedules.

SCHEDULE ONE - INCOME AND EXPENDITURES
(Six-month Summary)

INCOME			
SOURCE OF INCOME	**PERIOD**	**AMOUNT**	**COMMENTS**
Stipend	mo	400	Aug.
"	Mo.	200	Sept.
Scholarship	Mo	159	Every Month
Part time Job	W.B.	18	Paid Bi-Weekly
Food Stamps		66	Starting in Oct

EXPENDITURES				
TYPE	**TOTAL BALANCE**	**PERIOD PAYMENTS**		**COMMENTS**
Rent		92	m	
Light (Electric &S)		8	m	In summer
Credit Union	730 est	71	m	
Car Insurance		96	⁶ₘ	Due Sept.
Doctor		3	m	
Hospital Insurance		200	y	Pay Quarterly
Phone		20	m	Incl. L.D. Call's
Food		106	M	Food Stamps (40 Paid)
Personal Expenses		5	m	Not covered
Car		3	wk	
Misc		15		
Books		100		Full school year
Christmas				

SCHEDULE TWO

SIX MONTH CASH PROJECTION

MONTHS	Sept	Oct	Nov	Dec	Jan	Feb
BEGINNING BALANCE	50	166	54	(20)	(111)	(218)
INCOME						
Stipend	200					
Scholarship	159	159	159	159	159	159
Part time Job	72	72	72	108	72	72
Food Stamps	30	66	66	66	66	66
Total	461	297	297	333	297	297
TOTAL INCOME						
EXPENDITURES						
Rent	92	92	92	92	92	92
Light	8	10	12	17	20	20
Phone	20	20	20	20	20	20
Credit Union	71	71	71	71	71	71
Doctor	3	3	3	3	3	3
Food	106	106	106	106	106	106
Personal	5	5	5	5	5	5
Car	15	12	12	20	12	12
Misc.	15	15	15	15	15	15
Christmas				50		
Car Insurance		25	25	25		
Hospital Insurance		50			50	
Books	10		10		10	10
(By Month) **TOTAL EXPENDITURES**	345	409	371	424	404	354
(By Month) **ENDING BALANCE**	116	(112)	(74)	(91)	(107)	(57)
Cumulative	166	54	(20)	(111)	(218)	(275)

RECOMMENDATIONS

Rent: Move to apt. further from school which rents for $80 per mo.

Heat: Maintain a more constant temperature reading on thermostat. Keep the apt about 2 degrees warmer in the night and 2 degrees cooler during the day, so that the change in temperature is not too extreme.

Phone: Reduce the long distance phone calls. Make them on the weekend or after 5:00 p.m.

Credit Union: No change.
Doctor: No change.

Food: By shopping once a week and buying sale items the food bill could easily be reduced to $96 per month. Question — can this savings be converted to a dollar savings as shown on the budget?

Personal — No change.

Car: Since the car was just purchased no allowance was made for tires, maintenance, etc. for this six month period.

Misc. This reduction can be made by weighing each misc. item and deferring or eliminating as many as possible.

Christmas: $45 is a min amount. By giving homemade gifts and food (cookies or fruit cake) this should be enough. This is a $5 reduction from est. on cash projection

Car Ins: By paying it semi-annually, a savings on the service charge can be obtained

Books: Defer until next summer and use the monthly $400 stipend for purchasing required books.

SIX-MONTH CASH BUDGET

MONTHS	Sept ACT.	Sept BUD.	Oct ACT.	Oct BUD.	Nov ACT.	Nov BUD.	Dec ACT.	Dec BUD.	Jan ACT.	Jan BUD.	Feb ACT.	Feb BUD.
BEGINNING BALANCE		50		220		162		153		113		48
Income												
Stipend		200										
Scholarship		159		159		159		159		159		159
Part time job		72		72		72		108		72		72
Food Stamps		130		66		66		66		66		66
Total (Including Begin. Bal)		511		517		459		486		410		345
Expenditures												
Rent		80		80		80		80		80		80
Light		8		10		11		15		17		17
Phone		16		16		16		16		16		16
Credit Union		71		71		71		71		71		71
Doctor		3		3		3		3		3		3
Food		96		96		96		106		96		96
Personal		5		5		5		5		5		5
Car		12		12		12		20		12		12
Misc.				12		12		12		12		12
Christmas								45				
Car Insurance				50								
Hospital Insurance										50		
Clothes												
Total		291		355		306		373		362		372
ENDING BALANCE		220		162		153		113		48		133

* ACT. - Actual amount spent   BUD. - Amount budgeted in the financial plan

3

An Ordinary Couple

THE USE OF CREDIT can be compared with the use of fire: as long as they are both under control they benefit you but if they get out of hand, beware! A great majority of Americans use credit and most of them have been burned by misusing it.

As I said before, there is nothing wrong with using credit as long as you keep it in control. Proverbs 22:27 cautions:

> If you have no means of paying you will
> find your bed taken from under you.

This graphic statement sums up the care needed in credit buying.

There are many reasons for the misuse of credit, but one in particular is so prevalent I'd like to deal with it first. When a couple comes to me with this problem there is little I can do. I am speaking of the misuse of credit to supply a deep emotional need. In particular, I think about one couple who called me about five years ago.

Ron and his wife, Gail, seemed to have everything going for them: faithful members of their church, two young children, an interesting well-paying job for Ron, and a modern suburban home. But Ron charged every gadget that caught his eye and Gail continually charged clothes and cosmetics she had no need for. When they fell behind on their payments, money frustration set in. A good raise for Ron didn't help. Through bitter experience they learned they could not borrow themselves out of debt at a finance company. Tempers exploded over the lack of money. It looked as though their financial problems were turning a model marriage into a farce. Finally they came to me. During our discussion of their finances, Ron suddenly lashed out at his wife, "If you didn't spend so much on clothes this mess wouldn't have happened."

Gail retorted, "If you didn't lug home every screwball item you happen to see, we'd have enough money to live on."

The recriminations rampaged as each one brought up the shortcomings of the other. They left my office still arguing. Eventually they called a marriage counselor into the picture. In time, she was able to show each of them how their over-charging had been a way of getting back at one another for hurts, real and imagined. Ron over-purchased because he felt he never measured up to the other members of his wife's family; Gail did the same because Ron didn't have confidence in her. Dealing with their emotional problems was as important as dealing with their financial ones.

Eventually as Ron helped Gail to grow in self-confidence, it was no longer necessary for her to buy unneeded cosmetics and clothes. As Gail responded to Ron in a way to make him feel important to her, he ceased to be a buyer of every tool on the market. They came back to talk to me; their bills were unscrambled; and the four schedules were used to make their financial plan.

The combination of getting back to their church and beginning to pray again, sticking it out with their financial plan, and dealing with their emotional problems eventually saw them climbing out of debt and into a lifestyle that was rewarding to them both. Let me repeat, however, no financial plan will cure emotional purchasing. A family with that problem needs much prayer and usually outside professional help.

By no means are most of the people who are in debt ridden with emotional problems. Most of them are just ordinary people who have been wooed into overspending their income. In particular I think of Jim and Debby Crossman. They had no big emotional hang-ups. They were simply one of the millions of victims of the keeping-up-with-the-Jones syndrome, a syndrome that, in one way or another, touches us all.

Jim and Debby started their life together under the same financial conditions as many other young couples. Although Jim had a steady job, he earned a minimal salary. It was enough, however, to allow Debby and him to get credit from a bank and several stores. They began to enjoy an artificially high standard of living through the use of their credit cards.

Within a year they lost sight of their obligation to pay their debts and had set no limits on how much spending was enough. In a race to obtain status they became so overextended financially that memos from their creditors came weekly in the mail.

Soon phone calls asking for payments began. By this time Jim and Debby, who by now had a baby and another one coming, were under considerable stress, because they could not begin to meet their monthly obligations.

One afternoon on a trip to the shopping mall, Debby passed a loan company with a big sign saying, "Consolidate your bills! Why make many payments when one will do?" Going inside, she discovered it to be similar to a bank or department store credit department. Briefly explaining their plight to a pleasant young man, she was told they could arrange a loan for her husband and her that would eliminate their other debts and reduce the many monthly payments into one easy payment. That evening, explaining it to Jim, they both decided that borrowing was the way to go. They obtained the loan and paid their bills. Things went smoothly for them for about four months.

Since paying off the former creditors raised their credit standing, they once again were tempted to buy things they didn't need. Giving in to these temptations soon brought them to the place where they were again overextended. They found the cheerful loan company was not so pleasant when they missed a monthly payment. Worry and tension made it hard for them to talk about their problem. Jim resented every purchase Debby made for the family. Debby resented Jim's resentment. Bankruptcy was an idea that Jim played with from time to time. Leaving Jim and starting over again was an option Debby considered. At the beginning of their marriage they had faithfully attended church, but now even church was too much for them to handle. It was at this point they called to ask if I would be able to help them.

They sat at our dining room table and glumly presented the whole problem. Like most other couples they were both embarrassed and felt they were the only ones in the world in such a mess. To me this was a good sign, for the first thing a couple in this situation has to do is to admit to themselves and one another that they have overextended their buying.

As we talked, both Jim and Debby agreed to stop charging for the present time. Together they determined an amount

24

that could be paid each month to every creditor and we used the four schedules to work out a total spending plan for their family. The next step was the hardest for Jim. Contacting their creditors, he agreed not to charge any more on their accounts and asked the creditor to accept a small monthly payment. All the creditors agreed but insisted on receiving the payment every month without fail, no excuses accepted.

Debby told their relatives about the dilemma she and Jim were in, and was surprised to find they were most encouraging.

At this point I explained again that it was imperative that neither one of them charge a single thing, no matter how much they needed it. I also urged them to get back to church because prayer would be a vital part of their recovery.

Each succeeding month at a predetermined time, Jim and Debby sat down to review how they had spent their money the previous month compared to how they had planned to spend it. They then refined the oncoming month's plan and discussed how they would meet all their obligations for that month. This took most of an evening but was the tool that helped them both stick to their financial plan. In the recovery process they lowered their standard of living and sold a second car which not only cut out one payment but gave them some extra cash at a critical time.

The side benefit of working on their financial plan together was the communication it brought between them. They began praying about their finances: asking help and committing their problems to the Lord.

It took Jim and Debby eighteen months of no charging to pay off all their debts. It was at this point I surprised them by saying they could charge again. We sat down and figured out a clothing allowance for the family and a maintenance allowance for the house. I asked each of them to make one list of their wants (things that would be nice to have but wouldn't make any real difference in their lives).

I showed them that in their particular case they could charge $72 of *needed* items per month, but no more. At the end of each month as they went over their bills and paid them, if they discovered a surplus they could either save it or use it for something on the second list of things they *wanted* or they could invest it in something else.

Since Jim and Debby had never envisioned themselves getting out of debt, this approach gave them great pleasure. When I do their yearly income tax they are always eager to share how they used their surplus.One year they saved it for a luxury vacation and ended up using it to replace their washer and dryer. Both of them were so glad they had the money available that they didn't mind giving up their vacation plans. Recently they have begun banking a little each month. Sometimes they agree to send some of the surplus to a missionary their church is supporting.

Jim's salary has been raised several times since then and each raise upped the limit they could charge. Both Jim and Debby tell me that knowing their charge limit and sticking to it has been the key to success.

The most important benefit, Debby told me, is the blessing God gives her as she stays within her limits. She prays before every shopping trip for the right purchases and the strength to say no to her "wants." Each opportunity she has to choose between buying or waiting gives her a chance to rely on God instead of herself. She claims that choosing to spend no more than their limit has brought her closer to God than anything else in her life.

Jim recalled one day when he stood in front of the latest model chain saw and talked it over with the Lord. As he listened, the Lord spoke to his heart and strengthened him to make the choice against buying it.

There is no comparison between the confident, financially solvent couple that Jim and Debby are now, and the defeated young couple who desperately sought my advice a few years ago. They both say that the long eighteen-month period of not charging a thing was worth it, and agree that choosing not to overcharge has opened the door to financial freedom.

SCHEDULE ONE - INCOME AND EXPENDITURES
(Six-month Summary)

INCOME

SOURCE OF INCOME	PERIOD	AMOUNT	COMMENTS
Salary (Jim)	Weekly	218	Take Home Pay (after taxes & Deductions)
Baby-Sitting (Debby)	Weekly	20	
Income Tax Refund		385	One time only

EXPENDITURES

TYPE	TOTAL BALANCE	PERIOD PAYMENTS		COMMENTS
House	19,623	196		Incl Tax & Ins
Medical Ins.		18		Bal Paid by Empl.
Phone		10		
Heat		30		Equal Pay all year
Light		40		Every other month
Water, Sewer, Garbage		16; 15; 6		Quarterly
T.V. Payments	86	10		
Dept Store #1	258	26		10% of Bal (1-mo Behind)
Dept Store #2	391	25		Contract (2-mo Behind)
Dept Store #3	172	17		10% of Bal
Bank Card	264	26		10% of Bal (1 mo Behind)
Gas Stations	125	10		Tools & Misc.
Car Payments	921	140		
Finance Co.	1465	125		Consolidation (1 mo Behind)
Car Insurance		225		Semi-annual
Life Insurance		35		month
Repairs and Clothes		70		month
Entertainment		40		month
Living		75		weekly
Contributions		95		10% of Take Home
Other		50		month
Christmas		400		Total Extra Needed

SIX MONTH CASH PROJECTION

	Oct	Nov	Dec	Jan	Feb	Mo
BEGINNING BALANCE	115					
INCOME						
Salary (take home pay)	1090	872	1090	872	872	87
Baby-Sitting	100	80	100	80	80	8
Tax Refund						(38
TOTAL INCOME	1305	952	1190	952	952	13:
Number of Pay days	5	4	5	4	4	4
EXPENDITURES House	196	196	196	196	196	19
Medical Ins.	18	18	18	18	18	1:
Phone	10	10	10	10	10	1C
Heat & Lights	30	70	30	70	30	7C
Water, Sewer, Garbage	16	15	6	16	15	6
T.V. Payments	10	10	10	10	10	1C
Dept. Stores #1, #2, #3	144	64	60	57	53	5
Bank card	52	21	19	17	16	14
Gas Stations	49	10	10	10	10	1C
Car Payments	140	140	140	140	140	14C
Finance Co.	125	125	125	125	125	12
Car Ins. + Life Ins.	35	35	35	35	35	26
Repairs and Clothes	70	70	70	70	70	7
Entertainment	40	40	40	40	40	4
Living	375	300	375	300	300	3C
Contributions	95	95	95	95	95	9
Other	50	50	50	50	50	5
Christmas		250	150			
TOTAL EXPENDITURES	1455	1519	1439	1259	1213	14.
(Monthly) **ENDING BALANCE**	(150)	(567)	(249)	(307)	(261)	(13
Cumulative Bal.	(150)	(717)	(966)	(1273)	(1534)	(16

RECOMMENDATIONS

First Attempt

Heat: Turn off heat in bedrooms. Reduce thermostat by 5 degrees. Savings $8 per month.

Lights: Turn off lights not needed. Reduce use of utilities. Savings: $5 per bill.

Repairs and Purchase only necessary clothing.
Clothes: No major repairs. Savings $30 per mo.

Entertainment: Limit to one evening a month. Savings: $25.

Living: Reduce by 15%. Savings: $45 or $56 per month.

Christmas: Reduce number of gifts. Buy less expensive items. Agree how much to spend for each other. Savings $150.

Total Savings Realized on first Attempt: $835.

Second Attempt: Reduce payments on charge accounts by getting creditors to agree to smaller payments. Semi-annual Car insurance to be spread over three months, which will defer $150. into the next budget period.

Savings Realized on Second Attempt:

Dept. Store #1	$30.
Dept. Store #2	105.
Bank Card	69.
Gas	29.
Car payments	240.
Finance Co.	210.
Car Insurance	150.

Total Savings Realized on Second Attempt: $833.

SIX-MONTH CASH BUDGET

Prepared after "Second Attempt" Recommendations

MONTHS	Oct ACT.	Oct BUD.	Nov ACT.	Nov BUD.	Dec ACT.	Dec BUD.	Jan ACT.	Jan BUD.	Feb ACT.	Feb BUD.	Mar ACT.	Mar BUD.
BEGINNING BALANCE		115		190		(18)		(54)		(154)		167
Salary Attips		1090		872		1090		872		872		872
Retas. Attips		100		80		100		80		80		80
Tot. Rec. and Int. Inc.										385		
Total Income		1305		1142		1172		898		1181		1119
House		194		196		196		196		196		196
Medical Ins.		18		18		18		18		18		18
Phon		10		10		10		10		10		10
Elet		22		22		22		22		22		22
Light		135		135				35				35
Water, Sewer, Garbage		16		15		6		16		15		6
TV Payments		10		10		10		10		10		10
Dept Store #1		22		23		21		19		17		15
Dept Store #2		15		15		15		15		15		15
Dept Store #3		17		16		14		13		11		10
Auto Gas		20		10		10		10		10		10
Gas Station		20		10		10		10		10		10
Car Payments/Ins.		100		100		100		100		100		100
Insurance Co.		90		90		90		90		90		90
Car Insurance												75
Life Insurance		35		35		35		35		35		35
Clothes and Shoes		40		40		40		40		40		40
Entertainment		15		15		15		15		15		15
Living		319		255		319		255		255		255
Contributions		95		95		95		95		95		95
Other		50		50		50		50		50		50
Christmas						150						
Total Expenditures		1115		1110		1226		1024		1044		1112

4
People in Trouble

A FINANCIAL PLAN IS NOT A TOOL only for those who have a regular salary and find themselves in debt. I've seen it used in many ways: a couple found out why they couldn't save money, a family was able to manage for the nine months that the husband was out of work, a divorced woman with small children was helped to manage in a desperate situation.

When I first met Jerry and Rose Schaeffer, he was a sales representative with a well-paying job. He and Rose lived with their two small children in an apartment complex which housed several other couples in the same age bracket. Their main goal was to buy a home in the suburbs. I could tell Rose knew exactly what she wanted when we began to discuss their financial plan and budget. She had a certain type of house picked out in any one of three areas. Jerry was also enthusiastic about buying a house. Both of them wanted to save enough money to make the purchase possible. They should have been able to save at very least $200 a month on the basis of Jerry's income compared to their normal expenses, but instead they realized they were getting deeper in debt each month. We approached making a financial plan in the usual way.

First, we listed all the sources of income they had. Next we listed their expenses and then made a six-month forecast. Reviewing the forecast to recommend changes in their spending I could see there should be no major problems.

Given their salary and financial obligations, I showed them how they could save enough for a down payment on a home in a relatively short while. About three months later Rose called and said they had only saved a few dollars and she didn't know what the matter was. She wanted to know how soon they could come over and talk about it.

While sitting around our dining room table leafing through

their money schedules, Jerry suddenly became defensive "The only thing I can figure is that you made a mistake on the plan."

"Could be," I admitted. "Let's see where it's off and maybe we can fix it." We went over the past three months' activity and checked it against their checkbook. When we were through, we discovered that Jerry had unknowingly spent the extra money. In other words, he had a cash leakage problem.

The first thing I pointed out was that he wasn't putting all his money in the bank, which is essential to accurate financial records. Then second, he often cashed twenty- or thirty- dollar checks to cover miscellaneous expenses. Embarrassed, he protested that he hadn't purchased a single unnecessary item.

After some discussion, he agreed that for the next three months he would carry a small notebook with him and write down every item he spent money on, things as small as a candy bar. Rose agreed to do the same thing. We planned to get together at the end of each month to discuss their spending. This way they would not only have a complete record of all their spending but could talk it over together and give each other moral support.

At the end of the first week, Jerry found he had spent eight dollars more than he estimated on lunches. In addition, coffee breaks and miscellaneous snacks were $3 over his estimate. He had also purchased a four-dollar utility knife and a nine-dollar nut and bolt storage bin. He was already $24 over his plan! He did better the next week and the week after that, but in the fourth week he spent about $40 extra. At the end of the month when we got together he had spent almost $80 more than he planned.

When we saw this he agreed that his spending was part of their financial problem and he started to watch it more closely.

Once Jerry and Rose began to account for each penny spent they started to save money every month and are now living in Rose's dream house, furnished just the way she imagined!

Although the word "choose" never actually came up in our conversations, what actually happened was that Jerry made a choice either to spend or to save. His choice affected his entire family and lifestyle.

George Kent was a senior draftsman with eight years of service with a large aerospace firm. For quite a while he'd had no eal financial problem. When a lay-off notice came, George was shocked but felt his ability and experience would enable him to find another job within the company. Unfortunately, here were no openings for senior draftsmen.

A look at the job market showed him it could be four or even five months before he could find another job in his field. George foresaw two major problems: first, he would have to get another job, and second, his family would have to reduce its living expenses. During this period, family habits would need complete revision.

There were several things George and his family could do to conserve money, some insignificant and others drastic, but all would help reduce cash outflow. The amount of reduction depended on how well the family followed through on each suggested cutback.

The first thing George did was to list every item that required a cash payment during the next six months. Below that he listed his expected cash income from all sources including the loan value of life insurance policies and emergency funds. The difference between the two lists was the amount George and his family would have to reduce their spending.

If George got another job within one or two months there would be comparatively little hardship on his family. However, if it took longer, or if he had to take a lesser salary, some adjustments in spending would have to be made.

Looking at each item of expense, here are some reductions George could immediately make:

Type of Expense	Present Monthly Amount	Monthly Reduction Needed	Method of Obtaining Reduction
House payment	$180	0	No action to be taken for 5 months.
Car payment	90	0	No action. Use as collateral for loan if unemployment continues.
Life & med. ins.	60	0	No action should be taken.
Phone	15	7	Remove extension phone.
Lights	25	5	Use only *necessary* lights and utilities.

Heat	30	8	Turn off heat in bedrooms and reduce heat in other rooms two to five degrees.
Gas & oil for cars	40	15	Only use car for necessities. No transportation required to and from work.
Furniture time contract	35	0	No action. Refinance if unemployment continues.
Revolving credit-A	20	10	Make special arrangements with each store to have monthly payments reduced and extend time required to pay off balance.
Revolving credit-B	15	5	
Revolving credit-C	20	10	
Contributions and charity	130	105	Reduce to 10 percent of unemployment compensation.
Milk	25	25	Stop delivery. Substitute powdered milk purchased with grocery money.
Groceries	200	120	Approximate savings through the use of food stamps: $100 a month.

An additional $20 savings could be made by revising eating habits: eliminate meat two or three times a week, use oatmeal for breakfast, reduce amount of portions served at the main meal, and shop for day-old bread and pastry.

Entertainment	25	10	Reduce but do not completely elimi-nate.
Misc. cash items	20	5	General reduction of activities by 25%.
Cash reserves	25	25	Temporarily defer.
Total	$995	$350	Monthly cash expen-ditures after revi-sion: $605

By implementing the above reductions George and his family could get by for about three-and-one-half months on his lump sum payoff and unemployment compensation. If he was unemployed longer they could borrow money on his life insurance, use their savings, and then take further measures toward reducing the cash expenditures.

George was out of work for nine months. During this time he received several job offers that would require him to relocate to different areas of the country, but he and his family felt they would stay where they were as long as possible. He also had two offers that were for substantially less money than his old job. Both of these prospective jobs required that he make a firm commitment to stay with them even if his old job in the aerospace industry reopened. George would not do this.

He did several things during this long period of unem-ployment besides reduce costs. He worked as a cook in a fast service restaurant for several months. During harvest season he picked fruit. His wife, Carol, got a job in a local depart-ment store. His son turned over his earnings from a paper route to the family budget. George was able to get some short part-time jobs as a draftsman in local companies. What he wanted, and ultimately got, was a job in his old firm com-parable to his previous one. After going back to work, he re-evaluated his unemployment.

"I knew I could get another job in a different part of the country but my family and I like this area, so we decided to stay here if at all possible. I also knew I would not be happy in a lower-paying job so I turned down two of them. However, if I had been out of work much longer I would have taken a job that paid less. My family was wonderful, we prayed a lot and are closer to God and each other than we were before. Although several of my friends felt I should have taken the lower-paying job and quit when a better one came by, that just didn't seem like the way to do it. I'm convinced now I was right."

The key to getting along for nine months without his usual salary was in the financial planning that George did. If he hadn't written down where he could cut costs, I'm certain the outcome would have been devastating. His lump sum payoff from his job and the extra money from odd jobs would have been viewed as a windfall and used for extras instead of money needed to meet the family's current expenses.

George made several significant choices. He chose to write out his financial situation. He chose to cut his spending. He chose not to accept a job that he knew he would eventually leave when something better came along. Today he is as secure financially as ever.

Charlotte's home was backyard-to-backyard with ours. She and Pat were good friends and *koffeeklatche* neighbors. When Charlotte's husband demanded a divorce, almost the first thing Charlotte did was come over for coffee. Pat poured two cups but they were too upset to drink it or even talk to one another.

When the divorce was finalized, Charlotte had custody of her four children and was to receive child support money; she had the house but had to make house payments; she did not have to pay the back bills but could not get credit anywhere. She had no other sources of income. She had the option of going to work if a job was available, or earning money in her own home. She initially chose the latter course and was soon babysitting, sewing, and even baking things to earn money. She kept track of every penny earned and spent, and was able to maintain a home for herself and the children.

Many evenings she came over for help with her financial plan. Since she loved numbers she was always eager to look ahead. The plans showed her how many hours of ironing, how many hours of babysitting, and how many odd jobs she'd need to make ends meet.

We shared with her the difficulties of raising four young children alone. She relied on the Lord in a deeper way than anyone I'd met. Day by day she stuck it out, knowing that if

36

she did two more hours of sewing or baked an extra wedding cake she would manage until next week.

The choices she made to keep to her financial plan were numerous. They involved choosing to walk instead of spending ten cents on bus fare; choosing to make soup for dinner instead of buying something more to her liking; choosing to make phone calls and write letters at Christmas time instead of sending gifts; choosing in every situation the least expensive course.

Eventually, as the children grew older and somewhat self-sufficient, she found a job, put herself through college, and today is working in a well-paid, challenging position as a special education teacher. Recently she said to Pat, "I'm never too torn up by the hardships I see my students and their parents facing, because I know that out of hardships, with God's help, comes strength that can be found nowhere else."

Besides the obvious, I think there is another lesson to be learned from both George Kent and Charlotte as well as Debby and Jim in the previous chapter. This lesson is that financial problems do not continue forever. They are either solved or some change comes that alters the situation. To the family who is struggling today I say, "Take heart." With a good financial plan and a few right choices you can end your financial woes. In fact, I would go so far as to say the time is coming where you will look back on your present situation and thank God for the lessons learned while you were there.

The last chapter in this book will show you how to make your own financial plan. Included are four forms or schedules for you and your spouse to fill out, and some extra helps to guide you as you plan.

As you work them out no doubt many questions will come to your mind. The next few chapters will try to anticipate those questions and answer them before you ask.

5

The Things
That Are God's

THE RICH YOUNG MAN WHO CAME to Jesus asking what he must do to possess eternal life was told he must keep the commandments. When he asked which ones, Jesus detailed them for him. Evidently not feeling satisfied with this answer he replied, "I have kept all these from my youth. What more do I need to do?"

Jesus answered, "If you wish to be perfect, go and sell what you own and give the money to the poor, and you will have treasure in heaven; then come, follow Me." But when the young man heard these words he went away sad, for he was a man of great wealth (Luke 18:18-24).

Jesus was not interested in having the young man's money. He exhorted him to give it away, then come and follow Him. What He wanted was a change of heart, so that the young man would trust not in his wealth but in God. If he had taken Jesus' advice, he would have been richer in ways he did not know existed. So it is with us, too. Whatever we give to the Lord, including money, He will bless and return abundantly.

We are told over and over by Jesus to be generous with the gifts God has given us. He seemed especially pleased with the widow who gave all she had to live on (Mark 12:41-44). In Old Testament days, and during the time of Jesus, it was common to tithe. We are told that when God appeared to Jacob and informed him that he and his descendants would own the land upon which he was sleeping, Jacob told God he would give Him a tenth of all he owned (Gen. 28:22). Later God told the Israelites to give the Levites, or priests, the tithes collected in Israel in return for their services.

In the book of Leviticus God tells us that all tithes of the land, levied on the produce of the earth, belong to Him (Lev. 27:30). In tithes of flocks or herds, every tenth animal was consecrated to God. Bad animals were not to be substituted for good ones.

I'm sure many people gave lame animals, took some of the flock or crop for their own use before determining what the tithe should be, or fell behind on giving it and said, "I'll make it up next month." When the Jews failed to tithe God accused them of robbing Him and He cursed them, but following His curse He offered them an incredible bargain that is ours today if we accept the trade God offers:

> Bring all your tithes into the storehouse. . .if
> you do, I will open up the windows of heaven
> for you and pour out a blessing so great you
> won't have room enough to take it in!
>
> Malachi 3:10, The Living Bible

So we have a promise that tithing brings spiritual blessing to our lives. This promise alone should be enough to start us tithing. But the promise doesn't end there. The Lord goes on to say that if we tithe, our crops will be large and guarded from insects and plagues, our grapes will not wither. The bargain is that simple. Tithing brings material blessing; if we tithe we can expect to prosper financially.

The Lord has still more to say to us:

> (When you tithe) all nations will call you
> blessed and you will be a land sparkling with
> happiness.
>
> Malachi 3:12, The Living Bible

As we obey God's direction the spiritual riches God promised blesses our lives; as our obedience brings us material solvency, those around us *will* call us blessed.

A tithe in today's terms is 10 percent of a person's income before taxes, before "emergency" payments or any other deduction. Tithing is not easy, and when finances are already in a muddle and bills are far behind, it takes a step in faith to do it. It's like walking into a deep fog in an unfamiliar place. You may feel that tithing is an imprudent and foolish step that may cause you to fall into a financial abyss. The only promise you have comes from the Lord, and these words in view of your situation, don't offer the comfort Scripture usually does. It takes perseverance to give 10 percent of your total income when the washing machine breaks down or you'd like to take a short trip. Most people in financial difficulties feel an *increase* of 10 percent of their income would get them over their problems, not a decrease! They can be assured, however, that God will be with them and assist them with their financial problems.

Dave, a friend whose wife had left him with five young children, was paying off a large debt. When he was laid off, he had to depend on unemployment payments and money from odd jobs to keep the children and himself going. One Saturday morning he stopped in and had a cup of coffee with Pat. After he told her about his financial situation, Pat suggested that he tithe. The next day Dave took that step of faith and put 10 percent of all the money he had into the offering at his church. Within a few days he received a call telling him his debt had been written off the books. Another call came, from his old company, asking him to come back to work at a higher-paying job. Looking back, Dave realized that, although God's promise had always been true, God had been waiting for Dave to step out with faith.

In my own case, tithing was not something that came easily. In fact, I struggled against it for longer than I'd like to admit. With a house full of children and always, it seemed, a new baby coming, tithing seemed too hard to do. At the first of each year I started anew and at the end of the year I would say to Pat, "We gave 8 percent this year," or, "Excluding taxes and medical expenses we gave 10 percent." During these years God was very good to us, but I knew we could and should be giving a true tithe.

The crisis that caused me to begin tithing happened this way: After we put earnest money on a home, two good Christian friends gave us conflicting advice. The house we wanted to buy cost twice as much as the one we were selling. One friend warned that we would not be able to make the payments and would end up losing not only the house but the equity we'd built up over the years. "God doesn't want you to spend money this way," she warned. "You'll be going against His will if you buy this house."

Our other friend urged us to step out in faith, saying, "God wants you to rear your family in an adequate home. (At this point we still had eight children at home.) Trust Him, He wants His own children to have good things."

40

According to our financial plan, even though it was a tight fit, the purchase could be made. So we went ahead. That winter there were so many unexpected expenses that we soon found ourselves financially in deep water. It began to look as though our friend whose advice we didn't take was right after all. In addition to a somewhat desperate feeling, I was also experiencing the humiliation that comes from making a wrong decision when I should have known better.

I could see that there was nothing to do except to take the Lord at His word. I knew there must be no backing away from tithing if I wanted to see the truth of God's promises of blessing. I decided to estimate what our annual income would be from my job (including raises), Pat's writing, and all other sources. Taking 10 percent of this amount and dividing it by twelve gave us a monthly commitment for contributions.

I included this in the top of our financial plan and promised that every month I would transfer it from my general account to Pat's household account to insure that I did not fall behind on paying it.

Needless to say, we did not lose our home. In addition to purchasing it we have even been able to take several family trips. Looking back over the four years since we began tithing, we find that our income has doubled in this short period of time, a growth rate we had never experienced before.

Even more important we have seen the promises of Malachi come to pass in our spiritual lives and the spiritual lives of our children. God has poured out His blessings on us in terms of time to be with Him, a new understanding of the Scriptures and praying, and Christian friends who add joy to our days.

People who tithe report an intangible "something" happens to their finances. They find they are not wasting money as they used to; they don't make bad financial decisions. As they walk in obedience to the Lord they find unheard-of bargains on just the items they need. Before they began to tithe, they had purchased bargains that often turned out to be white elephants. They say this doesn't happen any more.

A friend of ours told us this story. "I wanted to buy a new car because the transmission was going out on my old one. I was severely tempted to stop tithing so I could make car payments. As soon as I made the decision to continue tithing I 'discovered' a new mechanic who said the original analysis was wrong and the car could be fixed for thirty dollars."

Pat tells of a time she was visiting her friend Judy who raved, "Come and see what I found at the Goodwill store. Four brand new coats in the exact sizes we need for the children!" Pat was impressed and so was another neighbor who was also visiting.

The neighbor responded, "Judy, I don't know how you do it. Every time you go to the Goodwill you find exactly what you need. I've never found a single bargain there." Pat smiled to herself, knowing which neighbor was the tither.

In the same vein, Pat remembered another conversation between two mothers of big families. One was saying that people had blessed their family all winter with just the right clothing. The other was saying their family had received many boxes of clothing and there'd hardly been a thing in them they could use. Once again it was the tither who gave the good report.

How does this happen? Jesus has the answer for us. He tells us that if we give, things will be given to us, good measure, pressed down, shaken together and running over. This is quite a promise in itself, but Jesus astounds us by adding six more words that let us in on how this blessing will be given. He says of this material blessing, "Men shall give into your bosom" (Luke 6:38).

This means that it is humans who will provide the extra measure of blessing, which explains the bargains we happen to find, that repair bill that was much less than expected, the gift of clothing, the boost in salary when no one else received one, the return on an investment at an opportune time. As we are obedient to the Lord in the matter of giving, He allows men to bless us to overflowing. No wonder the life of a tither sparkles. Instead of stepping into the fog and landing in a hole, they find wonderful surprises around every corner.

Your contributions are an integral part of managing your money. Your financial plan should include an allowance for this giving. I highly recommend giving a full 10 percent (tithe) of your gross income and turning the rest of your finances over to God. He will make sure that all your financial necessities are met. You may not become a millionaire, or have your struggles eliminated, but with His help you will be able to overcome any financial difficulty that besets you.

When Jesus told the rich young man to give away his goods and then come back and follow Him, Jesus wanted change of heart, not money. Jesus knew this young man would never be a whole-hearted disciple as long as he had wealth. Jesus' request that he give it away was made for the man's good so that he would be able to follow Jesus with a trusting heart.

It is for the same reason that we are asked to give a tithe of all that comes to us. Again, the Lord does not need our money, but we need to take the step of obedience so that we can follow Jesus with a trusting heart. When we say, "Jesus, I give this 10 percent of my pay check to You, before I pay a bill or claim anything for myself," we demonstrate a heart full of love for God. Jesus, who so willingly obeyed the Father, will lead us into the spiritual riches which come to those who follow Him in obedient love.

6

Three Controversies

AT THIS POINT IT'S IMPORTANT to clear up a matter that bothers some Christians. The Bible states:

> Owe no man anything.
> Romans 13:8

People often ask me, "Doesn't this mean that having and using a charge account is wrong?" Maybe you wondered as you read about Debby and Jim why I didn't recommend that they pay cash for everything.

It is important today for Christians who desire to be good stewards of the money God has entrusted to them, to learn to manage credit. Already we are basically a cashless society. Some economists think a time is coming when currency as we know it will disappear and be replaced by electronic money. Paychecks and bills will be electronically fed into a computer that will keep track of each transaction. Food, gas, variety items — everything will be computed on a continuing credit-debit basis. If this were to happen, it would be vital to know how to handle credit. If you learn now, the age of electronic money will not push you into devastating financial debt.

In addition, there are other advantages to charging. It enables you to shop for bargains without having a large supply of cash on hand. It provides an accurate record of purchases that is nice to have in the case of defective or otherwise unsatisfactory merchandise. It is easier to take back or exchange an item when you have a record of the transaction. It also gives you an accurate, valid record of purchases for tax purposes.

Credit used as a purchasing tool can increase a family's buying power. Having credit available has averted more than one crisis. I remember a time several years ago when we were driving through the state of Montana with eight small children. The water pump suddenly quit. We were able to get to a gas station in a small town where a cheerful attendant notified us he would have to order a new pump from a parts store in a nearby city. Since it was Sunday the parts store was closed but he would call first thing Monday morning. If the right pump was available, it would be put on the next bus; the attendant would try to have our car ready by Monday evening. We had a limited amount of emergency funds, but by using an oil company credit card for the repairs and another credit card for the extra day's stay, we were able to continue our trip without financial agony.

Credit buying can also be a hedge against inflation. In some South American countries where there is a very high inflation rate people do not put money into savings accounts because it loses value too fast. They use their credit and all available cash to purchase or invest in goods that will be usable in the future. For instance, the price of an airplane ticket could double in less than a year. People who travel charge tickets as far in advance as possible to take advantage of lower prices. In our own country people hedge against inflation when they buy a home.

In addition, the proper use of credit reduces cash leakage. Cash leakage, mentioned in a previous chapter, occurs when you increase the amount you originally planned to withdraw from the bank in case you meet some emergency. It seems that if you have money in your pocket there is always a place to spend it!

Getting back to the Scripture, "Owe no man anything," I think it's important to realize that *to charge* is not necessarily the same as *to owe*.

When you go to a store and charge a pair of shoes you are not expected to pay for them until a certain date during the next month. If you pay the bill promptly, you do not owe anything. Failure to pay means that you have failed to keep your part of the bargain. That is where you are wrong because then you owe the store for the pair of shoes. I do not believe that God ever desires you to charge anything that you know will not be paid on the date due.

Financing a new appliance, taking twelve months to pay, is not wrong. You have entered into a contract promising to pay a certain amount on certain dates. There is nothing wrong with this as long as you keep your part by paying on time. When you sign a new contract, knowing you can't pay for it promptly, you are dishonest and wrong. Another wrong is getting so far into debt through charge purchases that you can't keep the contracts as promised. Be wary. Check with your financial plan so that you know your limits for contract payments. Don't depend on credit departments to tell you how much you can spend.

When Jesus told the parable of the talents (units of money), He said that the man who buried his talent should have at least invested it so it would gain interest. This tells us that it is right to use our money and credit for investments. The most usual investment is buying a house. When you sell a house it is usually worth as much or more than you originally paid. The interest you have paid on your mortgage has been in lieu of rent. A business is also an investment. No one invests in a business without expecting a return eventually on his money. A college education for yourself or your child can be considered an investment. A college graduate gets a good return on the time and money invested in education.

The general idea is that anything depreciating in value becomes a debt; anything maintaining or increasing the value of the money initially spent is an investment. We will cover the subject of homes and other investments in later chapters.

Two other questions Christians ask when they consider the Scripture, "Owe no man anything," are:

(1) Even though I'm trying to straighten out my bills I still owe many, many people. How does God view this situation?

(2) What about charging on revolving accounts where you don't have to pay for what you charge for 90 days? Isn't this a debt?

I would say that the answer to each of these questions lies in your attitude. God looks at your heart. Are you honestly trying to do what you understand Scripture is saying to you? Is your desire to get yourself as financially right as possible? If it is, then you'll know the answers to your questions.

Another point that is sometimes controversial is the subject of goal setting. I remember not too long ago when Pat said she wanted to talk over something rather disturbing she'd heard during the day. A woman who Pat admires for her fruitful Christian life had said, "I don't understand all this current

46

talk about goal setting. I don't believe Christians are supposed to set goals. Each of us should be able to let God direct our lives without making a lot of plans that may be entirely out of His will for us."

I knew why Pat was bouncing this off of me. She was thinking of the many goals we had set for ourselves in the future and was now wondering if we'd gotten off on a wrong track.

Looking back over our life together we began considering all the past goals we'd reached as well as the other happenings that had occurred without goals. Our first big goal had been my graduation from college. That had taken precedence over everything else including our social life and gatherings of the family clan. It meant long evenings of night school for me and putting the children to bed alone for Pat. But as we looked back we agreed it had been worth it. Another goal we'd shared was my passing the CPA exam. The course of study it took was exacting but we were willing to work towards it because we knew it was what we wanted.

Pat had goals for herself as well. I can still picture her holding her first check for a piece of fiction. "Can you believe someone would actually pay twenty-eight dollars for a story I wrote?" she'd asked.

Once she had had her first acceptance, her unswerving goal was to be a writer. Even though she received 144 discouraging rejections during the next year, she was not deterred!

Another goal we set, that apparently wasn't God's goal, was for me to open my own business. We planned, giving it much prayer and consideration. Three times the door was shut on our plans.

Another goal we'd had was getting out of debt. Over the course of time that it took, it was often difficult. We both grew bone weary of "making it do, wearing it out, cutting it down." We laugh now over the time that Pat was so glum over the whole thing that we went out to sit in the car and talk about it. (It was the only place we could be alone.)

She said, "I can't stand another minute of patching patches and measuring peanut butter so it will last until payday."

I'd done the only thing I could think of doing. I ran in the house and brought out our financial plan so she could see the goal we were striving for.

"If we can just stick it out until the end of summer," I encouraged her, "there will even be enough money for everyone to have new coats without any indebtedness." Because we shared the same goal she agreed we should keep on working towards it.

As we continued reminiscing we considered all the non-goals that had occurred. Although buying a house is a commendable goal for many, we had stumbled into buying ours. We had not planned to have ten children, but now wouldn't want to have missed a single one! It had not been Pat's goal to become an editor for Aglow Magazine.

As we looked back we saw how God had used my education, my ability as a CPA, and Pat's writing in His plans for us. We saw what a blessing our homes and the various neighborhoods we'd lived in had been. What an incalculable blessing our children have been and still are to us. We saw that Pat's work at Aglow had been a tool to bring His truth to many as well as ourselves.

It became easy that night for us to conclude that Pat's friend was only seeing one side of the picture. There are many goals that are worth planning for and giving priorities to. I believe God blesses these goals. Unless He says through circumstances or just the gentle nudge of the Spirit, "No, that's not for you," your goals can be tools used by God.

The next obvious question is, "How do you set goals?" One way is to get up in a helicopter in your imagination and hover over your life. Look down and see where you are. Look at your family, your spiritual life, your job, your finances, your home, your church and prayer community, and whatever else is important to you.

What would you like to see happening in each of these areas in five years? Write it down. Now, what will it take to make it happen? Write down all the ideas that come to you. They don't have to be in order. Talk it over first with your spouse, then include the children if the goal affects them.

Just for the sake of learning how to plan, let's say your goal is to attend the next Olympic games with the whole family. In order to meet that goal you'll need transportation, reservations, tickets, time off from work, and a special savings account. In addition you'll need a separate sheet of paper to figure the expenses involved. What will it cost? What are the possible sources of income to finance it?

Lesser goals might be finding ways for the children to earn

money to contribute, finding a travel agent, purchasing of practical luggage. Last minute goals would entail locating lightweight clothing, closing the house up, finding a dog sitter, and so on.

Each item needed to accomplish your goal should be *numbered* as you begin planning. Next you can add the date that you expect each item to be completed. The *priority* you give this goal should be agreed on by every member of the family. It could be that getting to the Olympics will be more important than eating out frequently or many other things. It should not be as important as church attendance and giving, children's school work, or helping with time and money when there is a real need.

A goal can be exciting to work towards. If you find that God has another idea for you, you can believe His goal is even more exciting than the one you made for yourself. Go ahead and set some goals, then work to realize them, under God's guidance. It could be one of the most Christian things you do.

Another controversy among Christians concerns the matter of savings. "Should a Christian save for the future?" we hear people ask. Often the one who asks the question quotes from the Sermon on the Mount where Jesus instructs us to lay up treasure in heaven, not on earth (Matt. 6:19). Then another Christian comes along and says, "But look at Proverbs 27:12, 'A sensible man watches for problems ahead and prepares to meet them. The simpleton never looks, and suffers the consequences,' " concluding, "Certainly this implies that we should be prepared for emergencies."

Once again the answer is in *attitude*. Is our money our own or does it ultimately belong to God who is the giver of every gift? If we see that all we have belongs to Him and that we are only stewards or managers of it, then perhaps the question of savings will come into proper perspective. To begin with let's consider the difference between hoarding and saving.

Hoarding is providing on your own for the future. Hoarding portrays an attitude of greed and a lack of trust in the provision of God. Putting money aside so you can be protected in the future is like saying, "I'm pretty sure I can count on You, God, but just in case I can't I'm going to store up this money."

Pat and I both believe that hoarding is wrong, even in small ways. Yet the temptation is often there. This last fall Pat heard that raisins were going to be nearly impossible to get before too long. As she stood in front of the raisin display she decided it would be prudent to purchase four times the amount she usually does so that just in case the rumor was true, she'd have enough.

"I knew I was hoarding," she said, "and I knew I was wrong, but it was easy to rationalize that I was doing it for my family and that made it all right."

But God had other plans. At Thanksgiving time the children came home from school and announced that they all had to bring some food for the poor the next day. Pat stood in front of the open pantry door and said, "Well, Lord, what shall I send?"

"Everything."

"Everything, Lord?"

"Everything."

Off to school went the soup, the fruit, the Crisco, the almonds, the ingredients for the Christmas baking and, of course, the too-plentiful supply of raisins. As Pat looked at her empty cupboard she felt she'd learned a valuable lesson. "Even though I was kind of glad that the poor were getting all those good things I felt that through the experience God had spoken to me. I hope I never give in to the temptation to hoard again."

To repeat, hoarding is your own protection against the future. Saving is provision for the future. When saving is seen in the light of future provision it becomes a wise action. I would urge every family to save money for major purchases particularly for a house down payment. I would say, save to meet your goals. Putting money aside monthly to prepare for a goal that you believe God has approved, is to be commended. As long as you remember that all you have belongs to God, then saving to meet a goal reinforces your effort to be a faithful servant.

How much is too much to save in a bank or turn over to another person to invest?

When members of the family are deprived of necessities so that money can be saved, it would seem that saving is taking too high a priority. A tithe should be given before any saving or investment program is begun. If a savings account or an investment portfolio ever becomes a source of pride or turns into a subtle type of hoarding for the future, then you have gone too far. If either one becomes a god in which you trust more than you trust God the Father, then it is not too drastic to consider giving it all away. If your investments ever begin consuming large amounts of time or causing anguish, then your perspective has taken a wrong turn.

Some people save only to give back as the Lord directs. Herb and Ruthie received, what was for them, a large sum of money they felt they could get along without. Herb prayed, "What will we do with it, Lord?"

"Put it in the bank and I will instruct you."

Three times in the next few months the Lord brought across the path of this Christian couple people who were in dire need. Each time Herb was instructed to give a portion of that money.

In hearing this story we wondered about his family. Herb makes a modest salary as a fireman. Was it fair to give all that savings away? Yet who can say? Shortly after the money was gone Herb and Ruthie found themselves planning a full-scale wedding for their daughter. The church was filled with flowers, the bride's dress was traditionally gorgeous, even the littlest boys in the family were resplendent in rented tuxedos.

"I'm not quite sure how it happened," Ruthie told Pat, "but we didn't have to charge anything or borrow any money at all. One way or another everything was provided."

I'm not quite sure how it happened either, but I do know God blesses those who live the whole of their lives trusting in Him. Christians should indeed save. Joseph stored enough grain to provide for the land of Egypt through seven years of famine. But our savings should always reflect the attitude that our money belongs to God. He has made us stewards of all He has given us. We can save while at the same time looking to the Lord Himself for our protection and provision.

7

When A Husband Dies

LAST FALL PAT AND I WERE FLYING across the country on our way to a convention when I said to her, "Our income tax refund this year won't be as large as last year's."

"Oh, really?" she responded, hardly looking up from her magazine. Being married to an accountant has conditioned her to this type of discussion.

I gave her a comparison of our anticipated income for the year with last year's income and proceeded to do the same with each category of expense.

This was the start of a little game I play every year. I estimate my income tax in the early fall and update the estimate every three or four weeks. I am pleased with the estimates that lower the tax and disappointed in the ones that increase it. When I finally prepare my tax return in January I compare it with my first estimate.

Sitting back in her seat Pat replied, "I'm glad I don't have to think about taxes and things like that."

I looked at her in amazement. I couldn't have been more surprised because I always go over our financial affairs with her. She has participated in the preparation of our financial plan, has her own bank account, and is responsible for a large number of our expenditures.

Several years ago she expressed concern over the fact that she was unfamiliar with handling finances. She had always managed the food and household money but felt that was not enough. So in order to give her experience in managing money we opened a second bank account for her. Both our accounts are joint accounts. All our income goes into the original "central" account and from there I transfer our contribution money, food, household, and routine clothing money to the second account. Pat is responsible for maintaining this account and not only deposits the money and writes the checks but reconciles the monthly statements. This is a foundation

52

for her to assume total control of the family finances if necessary.

But now I saw my preparations had been inadequate. I realized how carefully a husband must plan for his wife in the event of his death.

There are three major areas a couple should discuss and plan for long before there is any likelihood that the husband will pass away. These are: what should be done before a husband dies; what should be done following his death; and what should be done about the day-to-day activities after he's gone.

The first thing a husband and wife should do is to have a will drawn up. The average couple has considerable assets and a will can safeguard them. The laws distributing assets of deceased persons who have no will vary from state to state, but in most cases the distribution of goods when the wife is without a will is different than what her husband would have desired. A man who recently died had his estate divided one-third to his widow and two-thirds to his nine-year-old daughter. The widow had to post a $50,000 bond and furnish the state with detailed reports on how she was spending the daughter's share. In order to comply with court requirements she spent money on legal and accounting fees, and considerable time and effort.

In another situation, a man who was separated from his wife lived with his sister. He died many years after the separation without leaving a will. The wife got fifty percent of his estate and the other half was distributed equally between the sister and four other brothers and sisters. A will would have made it much easier for the wife in the first example and enabled the man to repay his sister properly in the second.

When drawing up a will it's important to have a lawyer do it the right way. Trying to save a few dollars by using a blank form purchased from a stationery store will probably cost more money in the end than a lawyer's fee. Quite often a stationery-store type of will is declared invalid, or it will not have the proper wording to make the desired distribution of the estate.

In addition to establishing a will, every family should have some type of medical insurance, at least the kind that covers major expenses. The wife should be familiar with the provisions and required forms. In addition, proper financial provisions through life insurance is a must. The actual amount of life insurance required will vary but a reputable sales representative can assist in determining the amount and type of insurance that is best. In addition most companies offer their employees term life insurance at a low group rate. The man who says he doesn't believe in life insurance should re-evaluate his position.

Life insurance can be used to pay off a home mortgage, clear up debts, send the surviving wife and/or children to college, be invested to provide a monthly income for the family, or many other things. But it can do nothing if you don't have any. Every wife should know how much insurance her husband has, what company or companies it is with, where the policies are kept, and how to submit a claim for collection. It's possible an evening with your life insurance representative is in order, to give a better understanding of your policies.

These policies and other important papers should be kept together in a safe place. A wife should have access to wills, social security information, pension data, bank books, car titles, tax returns, real estate agreements, and other important papers. A friend of mine and his wife each have their own box. This will enable either one immediate access to them when they need them. Included in the important papers of a husband should be a last letter of instructions to his wife.

This letter can be a source of consolation and help for his widow. It can leave burial instructions and a list of people to notify. She should be cautioned against spending too much money on the funeral. It's probable that she will be distraught and money will be one of her least concerns. This, coupled with the fact that she received or will receive a seemingly large amount of insurance money, could cause her to overspend on the funeral. The letter of instructions can list life insurance policies by company, policy number, and amount. It can even recommend which options to take on the insurance policies.

An explanation of the forms required (if any) for the family medical coverage should also be included. The letter could even contain instructions on payment of bills, sources of income, and a summary of the family financial situation.

A second important category for a husband and wife to discuss is what should be done in the immediate future after his death. The following is advice for a widow, but I would ad-

54

vise every married couple to sit down together and discuss in detail each of these items.

After the funeral, when the friends and relatives have left the new widow alone, money matters may not seem too important to her. There are, however, some decisions that she will be pressured into making. However, she should not let anyone, even her children, force her into speedy decisions. She should submit insurance claims and any other benefits she is entitled to. Aside from that she should not make any financial decision that will impact her future.

One important decision that should not be made immediately after the funeral is whether to keep or sell the family home. Whether the widow lives in an apartment or house she should not make a decision on where to live for at least one year. Even though many people may give her helpful advice concerning her home she should move slowly. Once she moves from the family home and neighborhood she cannot go back. There may be a strong desire to get away from the memories and reminders of her late husband and their former way of life. Selling the home may seem like the best way there is to solve the problem. Rather than doing this she should consider an extended trip or visit with her relatives.

There are many reasons why waiting a year to make an irreversible decision is important. "Time will tell" is not just a cliche but a worthwhile guide. In a very small way I experienced the benefits of waiting to make a decision.

When my family moved to our current home there were several large maple trees on the property. While I felt they blocked out too much sunshine Pat felt they gave much-needed shade. I wanted to cut down about three-fourths of them. After further discussion with Pat, knowing that once a tree was cut we could not replace it, I agreed to wait at least one year so we could see the trees during all four seasons. By the end of the year I had seen the value of the shade, so we did not cut any of them.

There are bound to be situations where my advice will not apply. Sometimes a widow must sell her home because of complete lack of money to make the payments. If she and her husband had recently purchased a home in a new area, she may want to go back to the old neighborhood where she has long-time friends. In every case the long-range impact of a home sale should be carefully weighed, which is easier to do after living in the house through four seasons under the new circumstances.

When a widow collects a large sum of life insurance it probably seems enough money to last for years. It could easily be four or five times her husband's annual salary before any tax bite. It looks like a windfall, a wonderful sum of money out of nowhere. Therein could lie more trouble than any widow could guess if it is misused. Her husband has not set this up for her immediate use but for her long-term needs.

Some simple long-range calculations will show that any life insurance settlement will not be enough money to sustain a widow plus children for a long period of time. After applying for Social Security insurance claims and any pensions for which she is eligible, the newly widowed woman should know how much money in a lump sum she will have and what to expect as monthly income. This information will help her in setting up a financial plan. In addition to matching monthly income with monthly expenses she is going to have to determine what to do with the insurance proceeds. A final decision on this should not be made too fast or under pressure. As long as she does not commit the money she will have a certain amount of financial security during a trying period of her life.

Options for the use of the money include, but are not limited to, paying off current and short term bills, banking it, buying U.S. Savings bonds, investing in stocks and bonds, paying off a mortgage, using it to return to school, using it for children's school, or several combinations of the above. Whatever is done should take long-term financial requirements into account.

The money should be put into a savings bank during the initial mourning period. All financial advice from friends, relatives, and the clergy should be set aside. She has to first set up a financial plan and then go to a reputable Christian stockbroker or accountant with her plan to obtain help in following it. Her friends, relatives, and clergymen can help her find the right advisor but should not advise her.

I know of a well-meaning son who talked his newly widowed mother into investing most of her $60,000 insurance settlement in a retail clothing store. He had been a manager of the men's clothing department in an exclusive store and knew he could be successful with his own store. He went over his plans so enthusiastically with his mother that she could not resist loaning him the necessary funds. He paid her a 10 percent return the first three years but in the fourth year the store went bankrupt. A disillusioned mother and a very sad son were all that remained of the legacy left by a hardworking man who thought he had provided for his widow.

A widow, particulary a new widow, should not invest in a friend's business. She should not buy stock on the advice of her relatives. She should not invest in the church building fund or development plans no matter how good and safe they may seem. She must be more careful than a married couple, and not make any investments or commitments that could cause her substantial losses or that would tie up her money so she could not get at it in times of need.

Another important project for a new widow is getting her important papers together. She should have ready access to car titles, mortgage papers, taxes, and so forth. This data is essential for making out tax returns, selling or buying a car, a home, and finalizing other major transactions. She should also update her will. Her estate is valuable, the disposition of it is critical.

Just as it was important for him to have life insurance, she also should have life insurance. She will probably not need as much as her husband did but she should base it on the needs and future requirements of her dependents. Along with her will and insurance she should have a letter of intent that outlines her burial plans, and where the important papers are, and any other data she would like passed on to her heirs.

One of the harder things a woman recently widowed will have to do, is to remove her husband's name from all records. She should go to their banks and have all joint accounts transferred to her name. The titles to the cars will need to be changed as well as ownership of other property. In most cases it is wiser for the widow to change everything at one time, including department store accounts.

As a woman begins life without a husband she will have to adjust to many things. Not the least of these is the complete responsibility for all financial decisions. If she had taken care of the family finances in the past, she at least had been able to discuss many problems with her husband. She can no longer do this. A partial solution for this is to have a detailed financial plan written out. This will help her to know how much she can spend and where her problems are. If she overspends, or had not planned for some major item she has a checkpoint to see what the impact of buying the item will have on her overall financial well-being. A financial plan will not be a cure-all but it will help with her finances and give her peace of mind.

The day-in-day-out activities of a married woman suddenly alone, are worth discussing. After Mrs. Cede, recently widowed, assessed her personal financial position she developed a financial plan that would help her and her two children live at only a slightly lower standard than they had before Mr. Cede died. They would have to get by on less, but Mr. Cede had planned extremely well for his death.

Mrs. Cede was eligible for Social Security payments because of the childrens' ages and she also received a monthly sum from her husband's pension plan. In addition she had considerable monies from several insurance policies. One of the policies was a mortgage insurance policy for the approximate amount of her mortgage. She took the money from this policy and put it in a special bank account. She transferred the monthly house payment from this account and so did not have to worry about meeting her mortgage payments. She planned to do this for at least the first year of widowhood since she did not know whether she wanted to stay in the same house. Along with the knowledge that her house payments were taken care of was the fact that she had greater flexibility regarding the future sale of her home plus an additional emergency fund.

She took a second policy and used most of it to clean up all her bills and outstanding contracts including a car and some new furniture. The remaining money from this policy plus the other two she had, was about equal to what her husband had earned in three years. This was added to her savings and investments to make up a complete portfolio.

Her savings account represented six month's earnings by her late husband. She did not want to do anything with it, but left it intact.

For several years she and her husband had invested in a stock market mutual fund. This is an investment company set up to pool the money of many individual investors to invest in the market on a large scale. The investments are actually made by professional managers who charge the fund an annual fee for their service. Mrs. Cede elected to stop contributing to the fund until she was sure of her financial situation. She put a portion of the insurance money in the bank and with the help of a reliable stockbroker she invested the remaining amount in good conservative stocks and bonds.

The annual income from her savings, mutual funds, stocks and bonds, added to her Social Security benefits and pension, brought her total income to about 60 percent of her husband's. This excluded the mortgage insurance which increased her total income to 80 percent. This enables her to maintain the same general standard of living even though she has to get by on less.

The first major daily-living decision following a husband's death is probably the hardest. After a major storm last winter a neighbor pointed out to Mrs. Cede some damage to her roof. She knew it would have to be fixed but almost panicked because she didn't think she could handle it. The worry and concern she had were much worse than deciding whether to repair the existing roof or get a complete new one. Questions such as the type of materials, who should install it and how to pay for it were being asked, all at the same time.

Finally she sat down and made two lists of questions: one relating to repairing the roof and the second relating to replacing the roof. She then answered each question and compared the answers of both lists. She decided to re-roof the house and chose a reliable firm for the job. They did a good job and several of her neighbors complimented her on the whole situation. This was the first step she took in gaining confidence in her own ability to do things that would have been done by her husband and helped her overcome one of the major problems of widows: having no one with whom to discuss problems and plans. While there is no substitute for a relaxed husband-and-wife discussion of a problem over a cup of coffee, Mrs. Cede was able to derive a certain satisfaction from sitting down and listing the pros and cons of various solutions to a problem.

Another aspect of the day-to-day business that confronts the widow is the inevitable con man. Just three days after her husband died a woman heard a knock at her front door. A sincere-looking man in a neat but slightly outdated suit asked to speak to her husband. Upon hearing of the husband's death, the man seemed genuinely upset. After a few moments of expressing his sorrow, he explained that her husband purchased a Bible with the family name engraved in gold on it.

He said her husband had paid five dollars down on it and was going to pay the remaining twenty-five dollars on delivery. However, he now offered to refund the five dollars in memory of her husband if the widow would buy the Bible. In a matter of a few minutes the emotionally strained woman paid twenty-five dollars for a book worth about eight.

Unfortunately widows, because they are so vulnerable, are considered prey by almost all con men. The following advice is to protect the woman who is alone: Do not ever take money out of any bank account at the request of an individual. It does not matter if he only wants you to do it to show your good faith or trust in him or if he says he is a bank official, police officer, undercover agent, government investigator, or anything else. No matter how convincing his or her story is *do not remove your money from your account.*

In summary, if a husband and wife will plan for his death, sitting down and going over the details together, the widow will be far more able to adjust to what possibly will be the most difficult time of her life. Once she is widowed she should plan to keep her present home through four seasons. She should develop a financial plan for her newly revised life, taking into consideration all her assets and obtaining help from reputable people such as her banker or investment broker. She should make her decisions based on this financial plan and not on the whim of either herself or her friends.

There has been very little said in this chapter about the part prayer plays in a new widow's decisions, but perhaps it was not necessary. There is no other time in a person's life when they find themselves depending on God so deeply as when death in all its certainty has made its appearance.

For many women, the death of a husband leads them to discover that:

Thy Maker is thy husband.

Isaiah 54:5

They find in God the help, the consolation, the friendship that is as real and comforting as their husband's. They find God Himself intervening in their financial problems to bring about solutions they couldn't come to. I've heard it too often

60

to doubt it, for the widow who chooses God as her husband, the financial problems will be the same, but the solutions will be touched and transformed by His mighty hand.

8
The Roof
Over Your Head

MOST YOUNG MARRIED COUPLES start their life together in either an apartment or a rented house. In the majority of cases they immediately start planning for the day they can buy their own home. Yet many people today find there are advantages to not buying a house and are content to rent or lease on a long-term basis. Several persons who lived in apartments and then bought a home have told me they made a mistake.

One advantage to renting is that it puts very little financial burden on the tenants. Usually the landlord only requires the first month's rent plus a deposit equal to another month's rent. The tenant may pay for some utilities but repairs, maintenance, and even interior decorating are handled by the landlord.

Another advantage to renting is the ease with which it is done. The prospective tenant and the landlord usually take care of the paper work in a very few minutes. No lawyer, real estate agent or other middle man need be involved. If the tenant finds the apartment through a rental agency there may be a fee but this does not complicate the moving-in process. If the timing is right a person could find an apartment on one day, rent it, and move in the next.

The ability to move from one area to another without making a large financial commitment makes renting attractive to many people. The effort of selling a home makes it impractical for people who relocate often. Renting an apartment or house allows a person to have a home situated to his present needs, not one suited to possible future requirements.

The consistent monthly costs of renting allow tenants to know accurately what their expenses will be. They do not have unexpected repairs like a leaky roof or exterior painting. Yard care and maintenance is done by someone else, which not only saves money but much time and effort as well.

However, there are disadvantages to renting. People who rent, often feel they are not members of the community in which they live. This is particularly true at neighborhood churches where membership is stable and many members have been attending for a long time. Apartments usually don't have much storage space or enough rooms to give flexibility to the home. After a few years most people have accumulated a considerable number of personal items and need a place to put them.

Many apartments won't accept children because of the noise and deterioration associated with them.

One other objection to renting instead of buying is that after years of renting a renter may feel he has nothing tangible to show for his money.

In our country the purchase of a home, particularly the first one, fulfills part of The American Dream. Once a young couple buys a home it is presumed that they and their marriage have matured. Friends and relatives bearing gifts come to visit them and extend their congratulations. It often represents a change in their lifestyle and spending habits. More time is required on projects around the house, more money is budgeted for repairs, remodeling, and upkeep.

When a home is purchased it is usually bought with the idea that the family will become part of the neighborhood and community. In that case a family will transfer membership to the local church of their faith and join in neighborhood activities, which gives them an opportunity to meet new people with a common interest.

A house also gives children a place to be themselves, where they can play without disturbing neighbors and passers-by. Teenagers particularly need a place to express themselves and bring their friends and still have parental supervision and guidance.

A basement or garage can double for a workshop, playroom, or storage area, while an extra room can become an office, sewing room or activities center. As a family grows in size and/or number there is an advantage to having a house that can absorb the growth.

One of the greatest advantages to buying a house is the sense of providing for the family that it gives the head of the household. Even though the payments are a major concern if the owner goes through a period of unemployment, a house can give its owners a sense of stability. Many older or retired couples enjoy the emotional security of owning their own homes. For many families on a small budget the equity that builds in their home may represent their only savings.

A combination of inflation increasing the value of their home and monthly payments reducing the mortgage result in the house becoming the largest asset many families have.

Just as there are disadvantages to renting there are disadvantages to buying a home. The cost of buying and selling can add up quickly. A seller must spend time and money getting the house in salable condition, particularly if it is being sold on an FHA loan. The seller must pay the real estate fee, real estate tax, title insurance, and escrow fees. He often gives a discount to the mortgage company. The buyer also has expenses in addition to the price of the house. He must pay an appraisal fee, a loan fee, escrow fee, hazard insurance and will often have to pay a portion of real estate taxes. The actual selling price of a house is impacted by the economic situation of the area. The buyer tries to get it for as little as possible while the seller wants as high a price as he can get.

Since purchasing a house is probably the single largest purchase a family will make it should be done with considerable care. After you have made the decision to buy then the next step, which is finding a lender, is of great importance to anyone who wants to be a good steward of his money.

This brings me to Susan Blaire. Few others I've met in the process of income tax preparation have yearly records so meticulously done as Susan's. It followed then that when it came time for Susan and her husband, Jim, to buy a house Susan really got down to the nitty-gritty of the financial involvement.

When she and Jim were married they agreed not to buy a house until they could afford it. They wanted to have enough money for a down payment, moving and closing costs, refurnishing and remodeling to suit their needs, and still have money in the bank. They moved into an apartment and set out to meet these goals. With amazing single-mindedness for a young couple they stuck to their plan and when they did start house hunting they were in a good financial position.

Susan, realizing how hard it is to save a thousand dollars, felt she should shop around for a lender rather than just go to the mortgage company the real estate salesman recommended. She went to nine banks, mortgage companies, and savings-and-loan associations and discovered the difference between the highest and lowest closing costs was well over a thousand dollars. Some of the variances she encountered were:

(1) Lenders who wanted to close the loan themselves but charged a considerably higher fee for this service than elsewhere.

(2) A penalty clause for paying off a mortgage early was sometimes included.

(3) Banks that charged for a credit check and appraisal and others who did not.

(4) Interest rates varied by ½ percent. A ½ percent reduction on a $30,000 mortgage over 30 years would save over $3,800 in interest.

(5) Some banks preferred a thirty-year mortgage to a twenty-five-year one. A $30,000 mortgage over thirty years at 8½ percent would cost $53,069 in interest. The same mortgage over twenty-five years would cost $42,525 which would be a $10,544 savings.

Susan spent considerable effort and several days researching and reviewing the data. When she and Jim bought their dream house they had a twenty-five-year $30,000 mortgage. The savings realized by getting the best deal in closing was more than enough to pay for their living room furniture. In addition, the shorter length of the mortgage at the lowest interest rates available will save them almost $14,000 over the life of their mortgage.

In addition to checking around for the best interest rate and closing costs, Susan decided to go one step further and do some checking on insurance for their home. She discovered that there was a range of homeowners' policies and she could buy only what she needed. She could also reduce the premium by taking a high-deductible coverage and assuming some of the non-urgent risks.

She did discover two additional important facts concerning home insurance. The first was the house should be insured for at least 80 percent of its replacement cost, excluding the value of land. Rates for policies with an 80 percent co-insurance clause cost up to 50 percent less than other policies. With 80 percent or more the policy will pay the full amount of partial losses; with less than 80 percent, only part of that loss is paid. Susan found that if her house was insured for 80 percent of its value and a fire caused $10,000 damage the policy would pay $10,000. If the house was insured for 60 percent of its value, the insurance would only pay three-quarters of the loss, or $7,500.

It was explained to Susan that even though she had insurance she would have to substantiate any claim for losses, particularly for household and personal property. In her inimitable way she felt the only way to accomplish this would be to keep an inventory of their goods, room by room, and update it every year. She developed a form for making the inventory, and she and Jim filled it out. She gladly shares her forms with readers who realize how much is at stake financially in a loss by fire, vandalism, or theft.

The amount shown in the "value" column should be the current replacement value less depreciation. Wear and tear of the items can impact the value.

GARAGE & BASEMENT

Item	Number or Comments	VALUE	
		Basement	Garage
Bicycles, toys			
Dryer			
Furniture			
Hobby, sports equipment			
Lawn mower, garden tools			
Sewing machine			
Tools, power equipment			
Trunks			
Washing machine			
Other			
Total			

LIVING QUARTERS

Item	Number or Comments	VALUE		
		Living Room	Dining Room	Family Room
Air conditioner				
Bookcases, books				
Chairs				
Clocks				
Couch or sofa				
Desk, contents				
Drapes, curtains				
Electric utensils				
Fireplace fixtures				
Lamps				
Mirrors				
Musical instruments				
Pictures				
Plants				
Radios				
Rugs				
Silver, china, glassware				
Stereo, records				
Tables				
Tablecloths, napkins				
Tape recorder, tapes				
TV				
Other				
Total				

BEDROOMS

Item	Number or Comments	VALUE		
		Master Bedroom	Second Bedroom	Study
Beds, mattresses and springs				
Blankets, bedding				
Bookcases, books				
Chests				
Clocks				
Desks, contents				
Draperies, curtains				
Dressers				
Filing cabinets, contents				
Lamps				
Pictures, mirrors				
Rugs				
TV, radio				
Vanity sets				
Other				
Total				

KITCHEN

Item	Number or Comments	VALUE
		Kitchen
Brooms, mops, cleaning aids		
Cabinets		
Clocks		
Curtains		
Cutlery		
Dishes, silverware		
Dishwasher		

Electrical appliances		
Freezer, contents		
Pots, pans, etc.		
Refrigerator		
Stove		
Tables, chairs		
Vacuum cleaner		
Other		
Total		

PERSONAL

Item	Number or Comments	VALUE	
		Jim	Susan
Cameras			
Coats, jackets			
Dentures			
Electric razors, hair dryers			
Furs			
Glasses, contacts			
Gloves			
Jewelry, watches			
Neckties, belts			
Rainwear, umbrellas			
Shoes			
Shirts, blouses			
Slacks, skirts			
Socks, underwear			
Suits, dresses			
Sweaters			
Other			
Total			

These forms can be modified to fit an individual family's needs. I believe every family should have such an inventory that is periodically updated. The ideal list would be even more extensive than the one Susan made and would include make and model number of the appliances, dates of purchases and even sales slips. Obviously this kind of list should not be kept at home but in a safety deposit box.

After the initial costs of homeownership have been dealt with, the next area of expense related to the roof over your head is the cost of home repairs, which can be anything from fixing a leaky faucet to adding several rooms to a house. All houses will require some repair, depending on the age of the house and the requirements of the owners. Today, many of these repairs are being done by homeowners themselves. This not only saves money but gives the homeowners a sense of accomplishment and satisfaction. Power tools, do-it-yourself workshops, and simplified home construction allow more people to do their own home repairs and improvements than in former times.

Two words of caution to do-it-yourselfers: Make sure you have the proper equipment and don't overdo it. A middle-aged accountant who sits at a desk all day is not going to be able to paint a house as quickly as a young mechanic who is used to being active during the day. Proper safety precautions and equipment are a necessity to doing home repairs yourself. A broken leg or missing finger is too high a price to pay for any improvement. Homeowners taking on repair projects should also be sure they can complete them. A professional called to complete a half-finished project may charge more than if he had done the whole job from the beginning.

Door-to-door salesmen, whether on foot or in a vehicle, often prey on those who are not careful with their money. One trick is to have a man who drives an old truck come up to the door and explain in a sincere way that he just completed another job but has just enough insect spray in his truck to go over the homeowner's shrubs and trees. He doesn't want to quit for the day just yet and since it won't take too long he will give a good deal and just charge for the materials. In addition, he says some of the shrubs around the house seem to be coming down with a disease that will kill them if nothing is done. After getting an agreement to go ahead with the job he will spray everything in sight with a dusty-smelling substance and then proclaim everything will now be all right. His customer may never know the material put on his shrubs did no good; it may have even harmed them!

Other types of home improvement salesmen to avoid are the ones with new, unknown products with lifetime guarantees. One of the favorite tricks of these people is to try and relate it to some reputable well-known item. "It's the Cadillac of garbage disposals" or "most plumbers recommend it" are some of the phrases used. An inferior brand of siding or roofing might be called "Continental Mark IV" and be sold at a high price.

All door-to-door salesmen are not cheaters, however. A few years ago a young man making the rounds in my neighborhood gave us a bid on painting the outside of our house and replacing the gutters and downspouts. He had just gone into business for himself and quoted us a good price. He was hired and did an excellent job.

It's a good rule to be wary of all high pressure sales people, particularly those who try to get you to sign a contract without giving enough time to think it over. Although this is standard advice, I learned it the hard way. During the time Pat and I were expecting our fourth child and our financial resources were at an incredible low, an acquaintance gave my name to a salesman. He called to make an appointment to discuss an important item with Pat and me that he insisted we needed for our well-being. He wouldn't tell us what it was but hooked us with the promise that it wouldn't cost us a thing.

Thinking we had nothing to lose we agreed to let him come. We made it late enough in the evening so that the children would be in bed, allowing us to give him our undivided attention just in case he might try to put something over on us. But our preparation wasn't enough for his slick sales pitch. He came, gave us a super-hard sell and we signed. In only a few minutes we had bought a garbage disposal that was about twice as expensive as any other on the market. By signing immediately he could give us $15 off, which would be the down payment. He said that he would not be allowed to give us this offer if we didn't sign that evening.

Pat reminded him, "You said on the phone this wasn't going to cost us anything."

He smiled and said that of course it wouldn't. If we would furnish him names of friends and acquaintances on whom he

71

could call to sell garbage disposals, we would receive $5 for each sale he made. This money would apply to our payments.

The next day after thinking it over and realizing that we couldn't do that to our friends and also realizing that we had no money to make the payments we called the company and cancelled the order. A business-like voice monotoned that the penalty for cancelling was one-fourth of the total price.

We took the agreement to a friend who was a lawyer and he told us that not only did we owe the money but that this company was noted for its collection practices. "You've no choice but to pay," he advised, "but consider it a lesson well worth the price." He related many cases he had seen where people had lost thousands of dollars by signing contracts without understanding all the details or reading the fine print.

Little by little we did manage to pay the money. But the whole experience was so painful that even today we are still reminded of it whenever we are confronted with a salesman who insists that the deal he proposes cannot wait for another day to go by. Today's laws allow you to cancel within a limited time but the lesson remains the same.

If you are like most families one-fourth to one-third of your monthly salary will be spent on expenses related to the roof over your head. Go slowly as you make your decisions. If you choose to buy a home, do as Susan did and check out all the available resources before you close the deal. Take the time to make sure your insurance will do what you want it to do. Buying your own home can be one of the most satisfying ways there is for a family to provide for the needs of one another. Doing it as well as possible allows you to be a good steward of the resources God has entrusted to your care.

9

The Car Deal

THE SECOND LARGEST INVESTMENT most people make is in an automobile, but, unlike a home, the value of a car goes down as it is used.

There are many uses for a car, which is one reason for the large number of models and types. The type of use and the amount of money you are willing to spend will be the determining factors when you buy a car. If it is to be the only car for a family which includes several children, the best choice may be a station wagon or sedan. If it's a second car used primarily for going to work, it could be a smaller compact. A heavier car might be required if there is considerable highway driving to be done. Younger people may want a sports car or a van.

If you are purchasing a new car, an additional consideration will be the accessories that go with it. Power steering, power brakes, and a radio are no longer considered luxuries. Air conditioning is a must in many areas. The desirability of such items as power windows should be weighed against the fact that every electrical "extra" cuts into your gas mileage. Another factor to consider is the timing of the purchase. There is considerable savings to be gained by buying the current year's model in the fall when the new models are being introduced.

The age and condition of your current car is also a factor in knowing when to purchase another one. After it has gone 60,000 to 75,000 miles, it will probably be ready for some repairs. After 120,000 to 130,000 miles it will be ready for a second round of extensive repair. My preference is to keep a car as long as possible to reduce the annual depreciation. It takes a lot of repairs to make up for this. For example, a $5,000 car costs $1,250 per year if you keep it four years, but only $625 if you keep it eight years. These numbers have to be

73

adjusted by the estimated trade-in value, but a car kept eight years will almost always cost less per year.

When buying a car don't be afraid to shop around and compare prices, models, and makes. A few hours spent at the library going over Consumer Research, The Kelly Auto Market Report (Blue Book) and other magazines will be time well spent. Most libraries have a wealth of information indexed and catalogued for you. All you need is an idea of what you want, some time to research, and a pencil and paper for note taking. You can usually find the good and bad features of the car you want and "book" prices.

I recently traded-in our old van with over 130,000 miles on it. When I first announced my intent to do this, Gary, my friend and co-worker, encouraged me to really shop around for the best buy possible. Thinking back to when he bought his car I knew he meant going to several agencies, comparing prices, models, and condition of the cars plus haggling with car salesmen to get the best deal. I had never really done extensive shopping for a car before. In the past I looked for the car I wanted in a pre-determined price range and then bought it. I wasn't sure I had the personality to try Gary's way. This time I knew I would have to do a little bargaining because the car I felt we wanted was a used, nine-passenger station wagon in good condition.

I started by going to the library to check makes, models and prices from the literature there. I then went to the bank to check "high" and "low" blue book values. High value represents the average retail price of model and low value is what the wholesale value averages. Car dealers like to buy at wholesale and sell at retail or better. The difference between these figures is the amount available for negotiation. After arming myself with statistics on several models I called some knowledgeable friends to see what they could do to help. Meanwhile Pat and I discussed our need with some good friends. They suggested that we take another look at the Scripture:

> Seek ye first the kingdom of God and His right-
> eousness and all these things shall be added
> unto you.
>
> Matthew 6:33

Our friend, Bill Bair, explained that if we were truly

seeking to make God first in our lives then we could expect to find the right car at the right price. "The Lord knows your need," he told us. "He will provide the right car as you are seeking to put Him first in your life."

Pat was the one who prayed, "Lord, I expect this car to come to us at the right time and the right price. I thank You for it. Amen."

The first station wagon that came to our attention after this prayer was through a friend who had a friend who was service manager of an automotive parts wholesale company. After several attempts, we finally got together so I could test drive it and look it over. It was a good-looking car but fortunately I had done my homework and knew that the price that was being asked was over the high book price, especially since it had gone many, many miles.

At the same time I called on several new car dealers, having decided not to go to any used car lots. Since I wanted a late model in good condition with low mileage, my best chance was with a private party or some dealer that had taken a wagon as a trade for a new car. The cars I saw were either in poor condition or were too high priced. My van that I would use as a trade-in was also a problem. Every salesman admitted there was a good market for used vans but not those that had gone over 130,000 miles, needed brakes, a new window, a new seat, and paint job. In addition it was too old to be listed in the "blue book." I insisted it was worth something because of the high demand for vans and was fixable. I was willing to give my van plus $2,500 for a good nine-passenger wagon with less than 50,000 miles on it.

After considerable looking I found a four-year-old station wagon in excellent shape with only 28,000 miles on it. I felt certain that this was the car we had prayed for. The dealer was asking $4,300 because of the low mileage and general condition of the car even though the book value was $3,800. After driving it and looking it over I offered $2,500 plus my van subject to a checkout by my mechanic. He disagreed emphatically but finally agreed to take the offer to the sales manager. He wrote it up and asked for a small check to show my good faith so I gave him $50 for deposit. Twenty minutes later he returned and said no to my offer. Since the car was in good shape and they would have to wholesale off my van because they didn't sell cars that old, they offered to sell for

$3,500 plus my van. I said absolutely no and started to leave. He said, "Wait, why don't you make a counter offer, one that is reasonable?"

I agreed and calculated a new offer in this way:

The low book value of the wagon was $2,950. Adding fifteen percent for a nominal profit, the lowest they would be willing to accept would be $3,400. I estimated the low book on my van to be $500 so if I was lucky they'd go for $2,900 plus my van. The new models had just come out about two weeks earlier so I knew that if I waited six or eight weeks there would be a chance of going as low as $2,800 if the car were still here. I couldn't go another six weeks in my van without making at least $200 worth of repairs so I discounted waiting. My counter offer was $2,700 plus my van.

The salesman looked shocked but after more discussion took the offer to the sales manager. Upon returning he sadly said the manager might consider $3,250 but no lower. Slowly I tore up my check he had returned and started to leave. He said there was one more thing; he had been working with the new car sales manager but the used car manager, who had the day off, would be back tomorrow and might offer a better deal. Since I was going out of town for two days I agreed to call back next week.

When I returned from my trip I found another station wagon and decided to compare the cost per mile of the two used cars with each other and the cost per mile of a new station wagon. I knew the older cars would have more repairs than the new one but higher interest payments, taxes, and auto license fees on the new one would offset this, for at least the first 100,000 miles. So using the price they wanted for each car, less the trade-in allowed on my van, I came up with a value of $7,000 for a new station wagon, $3,000 for the used station wagon I wanted (with 28,000 miles on it) and $2,500 for another wagon with 62,000 miles. The cost per mile for the next 100,000 miles for the new car came to 7 cents. On the car with 28,000 miles the cost per mile came to 4.2 cents for the remaining 72,000 miles. The car with 63,000 miles would cost 6.8 cents for each of the next 37,000 miles. These costs do not include the total cost of operating a car but represent only the initial cost. Since normal operating costs would be about the same, and I had made allowance for repairs, interest, taxes, I had a good basis to compare the prices of the three cars.

The following table shows the calculation I used for comparing the cost per mile of each car.

	New Car	First Used Car		Second Used Car
		My Offer	Dealer's Offer	
Cost after deducting trade-in (excludes taxes, interest, and fees)	$7000	$3000	$3200	$2500
Base miles	100,000	100,000	100,000	100,000
Less: actual miles	0	28,000	28,000	63,000
Net miles	100,000	72,000	72,000	37,000
Cost per mile (cost of car divided by net miles)	7.0¢	4.2¢	4.4¢	6.8¢

The station wagon at $3,000 would be the best buy. It would still be the best buy at $3,250, which was the dealer's last offer. Returning to the dealer, I told him I would go up to $3,000 but no higher. The salesman went back to the manager and offered me $3,080 as the lowest and last offer. I had come to a take it or leave it situation so after some stalling around, I took it contingent upon its being checked out by a mechanic of my choice.

The next day I reviewed all the steps of my negotiations.
(1) checked the models and types to find the right kind of car.
(2) read everything I could on the model I chose.
(3) went only to new car dealers after checking their reputation.
(4) compared prices.
(5) had the car checked by a mechanic.
(6) negotiated the price.

This brought me to the financing of the car. The salesman asked if I wanted to have it financed through his firm, but I said no, after hearing what the interest charges would be. I had already gone to two different banks and a credit union

77

and all three had better rates than the dealer's contacts. The credit union had the lowest interest so I went to them for financing. When I compared rates I calculated how much the interest would be over the life of the loan in each of the four places I looked. This gave me a real dollar amount to look at and compare. The credit union was almost $80 lower than one of the banks so there was no doubt as to where to go for financing. I did not even consider a loan company because I knew the interest rate would be exorbitant.

A word about borrowing money: Shopping around for the best interest rates when making a major purchase or borrowing money for any reason, can save more money for the time invested than most part-time jobs would pay. Bankers are amazed at the number of people who borrow from a finance company instead of a bank and pay three times the amount of interest. It's estimated that at least half of the people borrowing from finance companies could qualify for a loan from the bank. Several reasons are cited for not going to banks, some valid and some not. Many people are concerned over the privacy of their financial transactions and don't feel the banks will honor an individual's privacy. There is more red tape involved in a bank loan and often the impersonal image of a bank scares people. A finance or small loan company is in business to make personal loans. When someone walks in their door, he or she is treated like a customer who is going to make a purchase. Because of their past image, people going to banks to borrow think they will be treated as intruders. All such worries will cost you money. The next time you need financing go to a credit union or a bank. You'll find the people there are delighted to be of service.

The night I brought our station wagon home, the entire family raced into the carport to admire it. We all piled in for a practice spin around the block with our teenage son driving. Later that night Pat and I discussed the whole experience of buying the car. Both of us believe that the prayer of expectation that we prayed that night with our friends was more than instrumental in the finding of the right car and in my having the ability to shop around and make the best deal possible.

10

Day After Day After Day

ABOVE THE STOVE in our Navy housing-project apartment hung a free insurance company calendar. Instead of listing appointments in the spaces provided for the months of April and May, we had written what looked like a strange code. Beside each calendar number was a *W* or a *P* or an *S*.

Our friends couldn't help asking, "Hey, what do these letters mean?"

I would explain by telling them, "In less than two months I'm going to be discharged from the Navy with no immediate source of income. So Pat and I decided that we could completely pay off what we owe on the chair and davenport if we spend only $5 for food during the next eight weeks. Taking stock, we found we had large amounts of potatoes, spaghetti, and biscuit mix. Using them as a base we have planned our dinners for the next two months which will consist of potato soup, spaghetti, or waffles. We have marked it on our calendar to reinforce our decision."

Our friends were horrified; both of our mothers were thoroughly shocked. But at the end of May we owed no money and thanks to the free meals our friends and families provided we had managed to stick to our peculiar menu.

Looking back, I think that while the goal may have been commendable the means to achieve it was lacking in good sense. We had taken the idea of thrift too far. Without the aid of those free dinners we could have exchanged our good health for the $45 we used on furniture payments. Food is important to our well-being, our bodies are temples of the Holy Spirit. We need to do our part to keep them nourished and healthy.

It is for this reason that food has always had an important role in human culture. We read in the Bible how Jesus fed more than five thousand people with a few loaves and fishes because He did not want them returning home hungry. We read of the concern of the scribes when He ate with sinners and of how His New Covenant was given at the end of a meal and symbolized in bread and wine. When Jesus taught He used examples of yeast, sheep, vineyard laborers, fig trees, and sowers of grain. when His disciples were hungry they picked grain on the Sabbath in spite of the objections of the Pharisees.

Then, just as now, we find that day after day we must be concerned over food. Because of its high cost much planning should go into shopping for food and the preparation of meals. Impulse buying is probably the biggest budget-buster there is because in the grocery store we find a great many temptations to make impulse purchases.

Just as Pat and I erred in overplanning our menus for those two months, it is as big a mistake in the opposite direction: not planning at all. This usually happens because we get rushed. A rushed shopper rarely has time to shop the specials. Too often she (or he) purchases too much in the area of luxuries and too little of the items she needs to manage her household. This means that in addition to spending more money and not having enough items purchased for the week, rush shoppers either have to go back to the store or send a teenager or husband.

All of those options are less than satisfactory, not only because of the inconvenience to the person returning to the store but because it seems that neither teenager nor husband knows how to go to the store without buying a bag of cookies or some other item that ups the amount spent on food.

Over the years, through trial and error, Pat has learned that in order to manage her grocery money she has to plan ahead for the whole week and make a list of the things she needs. She uses ads in the daily paper and coupons to help her determine what to buy. Since there are two supermarkets near our home she found she could go to both of them in one trip with little additional driving or lost time. She compares prices at the two stores to get the best buy on non-sale items. Studying the unit prices convinced her that normally the large sizes are less expensive than the smaller ones although there are occasions when the smaller ones are less per ounce. Although each family is different, it's possible that some of Pat's suggestions for grocery shopping will be of value:

Always prepare a week's menu in advance and shop from a list. This will take about half an hour of time, but the savings may make it the highest paid half hour of the week.

Buy fresh fruits and vegetables only when they are in season. Figure out the cost of fruit, sugar, and canning supplies and decide how much savings there is before canning or freezing anything.

Use non-fat dry milk for cooking. For family use, if you have the time it can be mixed half and half with whole milk and still taste pretty good.

Buy day-old bread and store it in the freezer.

Compare appearance with price, e.g. are canned whole beets worth more than the same amount of diced beets that are less expensive? Are the redder, more expensive apples better than the not-so-red apples?

Use medium instead of sharp cheese. Purchase house brands instead of national brands when they cost less.

Give children snacks with food value such as granola, nuts, cheeses, fruit, and cottage cheese instead of non-nutritive potato chips, candy, or pop. Sometimes nutritious foods cost more but when health factors are compared the value is always on the side of nutrition.

Purchase meat on the basis of cost per *serving* instead of cost per pound. Buy roasts instead of steaks. Learn to substitute soy beans in the form of texturized vegetable protein (TVP) for hamburger. Extreme care should be used when beef is bought in bulk. Waste and poor quality often make a seemingly good buy a bad one. Usually meat bought during a sale at the supermarket is a better buy than meat bought in bulk.

Stay away from prepared foods or allow only one night a week of pizza, TV dinners, etc. These items cost *much* more than they are worth in food value.

If possible shop without the pressure of having children with you.

Do not shop when you are hungry. A friend of ours began spending 25 percent more on groceries and she couldn't figure out why. Then it occurred to her that ever since she had begun fasting all day Friday (her shopping day), her hunger had caused her to purchase more than ever before.

Another item related to food costs is the expense of running the car to the store. Spending a dollar's worth of gas to save on a fifty-cent special doesn't make sense. This is compounded if the total cost of running a car is calculated. So-called savings obtained from shopping at several stores, or going to the store several times a week for one or two items may actually cost you money and time. If depreciation, repair, maintenance, and upkeep costs are used to calculate the cost of operating a car, the resulting figure is well over 10^c a mile. This figure can be used to check the cost of driving to the drugstore for some toothpaste or the grocery store for a loaf of bread. (It is also a good figure to use when discussing the cost of operating a car with teenage drivers.)

In addition to food costs there are the day after day expenses of running a household. Usually this is an area where we can save by using a little self-discipline. One place to cut costs is the heat bill. Insulating the roof, thermopane windows, or fires in an enclosed fireplace or Franklin stove can all help but are not available to everyone.

Everyone can, however, reduce the thermostat. A cooler house in the winter does not mean everyone has to wear sweaters all the time. It can be done by reducing the heat in the bedrooms, turning the thermostat partially down about an hour before bedtime and not turning it fully up first thing in the morning. Reducing the temperature a few degrees when the house is empty during the day will also cut fuel expenses.

A leak in one or more of your water faucets is like a hole in your pocket. You are losing only a little bit of money at a time but it adds up eventually to a noticeable amount. If the leak is in a hot water line the money wasted is even more.

Light sockets should be looked upon as another kind of faucet. It doesn't make any more sense to leave the lights on in an unused room than to leave the water running in an unused sink. I have turned off as many as twelve unused lights in my home with no adverse impact on anyone!

Careful cooking and baking can also result in gas or electricity savings. Meat should be thawed, or brought to room temperature before cooking. Cooking utensils should cover the range unit on which they are placed. If a small pan is put on a large unit it not only is wasteful but is potentially dangerous. Make sure your oven door shuts tightly to seal in the heat. *Don't* use your oven to heat the kitchen. It was not designed for this function.

Your refrigerator and freezer can be cost-saving appliances if you let them work for you. The gasket or rubber strip around the door is usually one of the first things to wear out. Periodically check it, and replace it if it's worn. Putting hot food into a refrigerator or freezer costs money in electricity.

A feeling shared by many people is that if one is good, two bigger ones will be better. This has been the American approach to life and as a result a lot of resources have been wasted. Oftentimes when we put extra soap in the washing machine or dishwasher, or extra fertilizer on plants, we do more harm than good. Many stains on clothing are simply the result of detergents that have not been rinsed out. The rinse cycle on most washing machines cannot remove all the detergent if too much has been used. Over a period of time this accumulation will cause stains to appear. If these stained articles are run through a complete washing cycle without any detergent, the stains will possibly disappear.

The opposite can be true if too little of an ingredient is used in an effort to save money. Since most manufacturers test their products to determine the most effective quantities, it is best to follow the instructions recommended by the company. This is true of not only cleaning detergents but of waxes, ready-mixed food, and appliances as well.

One of the larger expenses of most families is clothing. Maximum use from clothing depends on the care given to it. Hanging up your clothes is a good way to extend their life.

Alternating what you wear from day to day helps the wrinkles to smooth out between wearings. Wearing the right clothes for the right occasion can also be a savings. Don't wear a good suit if you are going to spend any time at all doing something in the yard. One little spill means a cleaning bill and shortening the life of your garment. This is also true of wearing a good outfit while preparing dinner, unless you wear a cover-up apron.

Thrift stores can offer clothing savings and other challenges to an enterprising family. It is possible to shop at Goodwill, Salvation Army, and St. Vincent de Paul as well as smaller thrift stores to obtain the items you need. To do this, however, you have to be careful and not buy unneeded items just because they are low priced. You must know what you want and be willing to wait until it appears in the store's stock. If it is not currently available at the thrift store it might be there in a week or two. Thrift store shopping requires patience and the ability to spot a good buy. If you have the time, this kind of ˗hopping can be an exciting challenge.

On the other hand, if your clothing budget is not extremely limited, you may want to consider the words of a Christian clothing buyer who gave the following advice: "Buy one good outfit a year with matching accessories instead of spending your money for several mediocre items. It is better to wear the same good looking outfit over and over than to have several outfits that you never quite feel right in."

Obviously sewing your own clothing could be a money saver but only if you don't sew more than you need and if you wear what you sew. There are many home seamstresses whose bulging closets of non-wearables are mute testimony to wrong patterns, wrong fabrics, and wrong styles.

So we see that day after day after day there are numerous choices to make as we consider the food, clothing and living expenses of our families. We often talk about the cleverness of creative people in the area of arts and crafts. Perhaps the most creative of all are those who use their creativity to manage well the money and possessions God has entrusted to their care.

Many times people who want to figure their living expense wish they had a guideline to show them how their income should be distributed. If this is your desire, on the following page is a chart that you can look over. It is only a guide. In

84

every case your family's special needs will dictate the amounts that are right for you.

PERCENT OF AFTER-TAX INCOME
SPENT ON CATEGORIES OF EXPENSE

Category	Typical U.S. Family	Range of Spending (See Note)	Tithing Family
Housing	27%	24-30%	26%
Food	24	22-26	22
Clothing and general living	24	20-30	19
Transportation	11	9-13	11
Insurance and Medical	8	6-10	6
Contributions	2	1-3	12
Savings and investments	4	0-12	4
Total	100%		100%

Note: As family income increases, the percentage spent on clothing and general living, transportation, and savings will also increase while the percentage spent on housing, food, insurance, and medical expenses will decrease.

11
Living and Giving by Faith

WARREN BRENNING WAS LEAVING for work when his wife said, "Warney, there's no more food and no money left to buy any." Marlene and Warren Brenning had taken their young family of six girls and a boy to the East Coast to be a part of the then struggling Christian Broadcasting Network. Like the others on the staff at that time they received no regular salary. Yet over and over the Lord had provided for Warren's family. So much so that even on this particular morning when it looked so hopeless Warren knew deep within him that he could expect God's provision.

"Honey, what do we need?" he asked his wife.

Marlene figured that what they needed came to fifteen dollars. Holding each other's hands, they prayed, "Lord, we know You are our help and we ask You to provide this day for these specific needs." Letting go of Marlene's hand he kissed her on the cheek, "Don't worry, honey, we can count on God."

Driving along the streets of Virginia Beach in his battered car Warren mused, "Lord, how are You going to do this? The studio's broke, my friends are broke. Where will the money come from?"

Waiting for the light to turn green he ran his fingers around his collar as he thought of Marlene and the children at home without any food. The light changed and to Warren's great surprise, the cab in front of him backed up. *Crunch!* The rear end of the cab was halted by Warren's front bumper.

Both drivers jumped out and surveyed the damage; another dent in Warren's car. Red-faced and stammering the cabbie apologized, "I don't know what happened. I've never put a car in reverse like that in my life." He scratched his head. "This is going to look bad for me. Could I just give you something for that dent and call it even?"

Warren nodded, "How about fifteen dollars?"

When the light changed again Warren made a U-turn. He could hardly wait to see Marlene's face as he explained God's latest provision.

The unique thing about Warren's story is that it is not unique. Over and over I have seen God provide for His children who are living a life of trust. Particularly I think of another person.

Nettie Mae McCain had only a few dollars left when her husband walked off and left her with three small children. She used the money to pay the rent and then there was nothing. "Lord, what shall I do?" she whispered. The Lord answered that she should sell all of the possessions that she didn't need.

Nettie Mae took Him literally. She sold everything except the beds and a few dishes, pots, and pans. Taking a smaller apartment she managed until the money from the sale ran out.

One morning Nettie Mae stood before the open cupboard and tried to comprehend that there was *nothing* left to eat. Two of the children padded out to the kitchen and stood on either side of her, holding onto her robe and looking expectantly at her. The baby whimpered in her bed. Nettie Mae asked, "Lord, what do I do now?"

Nettie Mae heard the words, "Go out in the woods and there will be apples." Putting her two little girls in the stroller and taking her son by the hand she set off for the woods with a shopping bag draped over the stroller handle. Before long, there on the floor of the woods, she saw the glitter of apples in the sunlight. Some were red, some were green with rosy blushes and still others were a buttery yellow. She and her son stood for a few seconds and gazed at the wealth they had found. Then they gathered every last one of them and started for home. Back at their apartment Nettie Mae made the first applesauce she'd ever made. For three days she and the children lived on it, thanking the Lord.

When it was gone Nettie Mae spoke again to the Lord, "What shall I do?" The answer came in the form of friends who brought sack after sack of groceries and even toys for the children. So began Nettie Mae's walk of faith as daily God provided furniture, clothes more in style than she could have bought herself, even money for the laundromat. Whenever it seemed during that time that she was right down to the bottom of her resources, God supplied her needs.

That's the way it often gets in this special kind of walk of faith. At the end of our own provisions we discover it is God who provides. This kind of day by day dependence is called living on faith.

There are many Christains today who live on faith. These are the heroic men and women whose growth in holiness takes a shortcut as they look to God to provide their daily bread, literally.

Some are missionaries at home or overseas who must wait monthly, or weekly, for enough money to be supplied. Some are single women, divorced or widowed with small children. Others because of schooling, part-time employment, unemployment, large families and a host of other reasons find a great disparity between their basic needs and the income they can depend on.

If this is where you find yourself, rejoice, for God is allowing you to be perfected. He will meet your needs in a way that only He can do, in a way that will spell out His special and loving care for you. In this setting you still need a financial plan, if only to show you what you need to ask from the Lord. Jesus said:

> You can get anything — anything you ask for in prayer — if you believe.
>
> Matthew 21:22, The Living Bible

The person who asks in the name of Jesus for his specific needs is in a better position than one who is vague.

Our friends, the Bairs, have learned to tell their needs to the Lord. Bill Bair had only a few more years to work before he could collect an early retirement and settle down to doing the Lord's work. Instead God led him to leave the gas company and any future guarantee of salary and trust the Lord for his family's finances. So began a day by day kind of trust for Bill, his wife, Marilyn, and their children.

During the first year of their life-by-faith, Jeanne, their youngest daughter, came to Marilyn and said, "Mom, is there going to be turkey for Thanksgiving?"

"It's not in our budget, Jeanne, but if you'd like turkey, why don't you pray for one?"

After school the next day Marilyn met her daughter at the door. "Jeanne, did you pray for a turkey?"

Jeanne nodded yes.

"Well, come look in the kitchen." There on the counter were two plump turkeys surrounded by cranberries, dressing packages and even fruitcake. Some boys in a nearby fraternity house had heard about the family living on faith and decided to bring them their Thanksgiving dinner.

Another time Marilyn, Jeanne, and another daughter, Joni, needed winter coats. The winters in Ohio are severe and when your only coat is thin and threadbare the cold is even colder. Marilyn sat down with her daughters and prayed, "Lord, You know our needs, You know our finances. We need Your provision."

Not too much time had gone by when a woman came to the door with three winter coats over her arm. She was a little embarrassed as she explained that she owned a dress shop and these coats had been sent to her by mistake. She'd tried to return them but for some reason she couldn't send them back. Then the Lord had told her that these coats were for the Bair family.

The family oohed and ahed as they tried them on. All three coats fit exactly and were what each one had wanted. Today as Marilyn remembers and talks about their great need that winter and the Lord's bountiful answer, there is a lump in her throat.

One of Bill Bair's favorite stories of God's provision revolves around a boy named Lance. Lance had come to the Bair family as one of the many foster children who needed the loving homes provided through the Bair Foundation. (The organization Bill quit his job to found.) Belligerently, Lance had scoffed at the Jesus Bill tried to tell him about, growing tense and defensive over the mention of prayer. One morning Bill said, "Come on, Lance, let's you and me move that pile of dirt at the back of the house."

Lance groaned. Grumbling all the way he complained, "What we really need is a rototiller."

"Then let's ask Jesus to provide it."

Lance fidgeted self-consciously as Bill prayed, "Lord, Lance would love to have a rototiller to do this work."

During lunch a truck pulled into the driveway. The girls ran to look, squealing in speculation over why a truck was coming to their house. Lance, who typically refused to get caught up in the girls' enthusiasm, stayed at the table. Then Jeanne called, "Look, Daddy! It is a rototiller!"

God's provision was too much for Lance. He jumped up and rushed to the window. He stared for a minute and then turned to Bill. "Papa Bair," he exclaimed, "pray for a car for me!"

In looking back at each of these families at this special time in their lives, a time of trusting and growing and living by faith, it would seem that God who allowed these families such hardships had a greater plan in mind.

Today Nettie Mae has completed the schooling that has led her to be self-supporting. The lean times she experienced have made her a woman of strong prayer who is able to be of true spiritual help to those in need.

Warren and Marlene eventually returned to the West Coast. There, while his logging business thrived, Warren felt the call of God to take Marlene and the children, now eight in number, to Europe to sing Gospel songs for the Christians behind the Iron Curtain to encourage them that they are not alone. Only a man who had learned to trust in God could answer yes to such a call.

For Bill and Marilyn Bair the financial struggle is over. The children are reared and the Bair Foundation, although it still needs support, is "on its feet." Bill and Marilyn often travel now. They raise money for the foundation but mostly they encourage others with their living, vibrant testimony that God is the great provider.

For those who through one circumstance or another have been called to live by faith, the reality of God's provision is clear. He can be trusted. For those who have done it, the natural outgrowth of this walk by faith is growth *in* faith as well.

Yet, most people will probably never be called to live so completely by faith in such strenuous situations. However there is another type of faith walk that God calls many to. It also involves our finances. It is called giving by faith.

This giving by faith was the kind of giving that Jesus praised when the widowed woman gave her mite in the Temple, the gift that went far beyond the tithe. For those who hear the call of God in their hearts to give a special gift, above and beyond the call of duty, and say yes to that call, the Scripture is clear that they will be blessed:

> For if you give you will get! Your gift will return to you in full and overflowing measure, pressed down, shaken together to make room for more, and running over.
>
> Luke 6:38, The Living Bible

These Scriptures I've used before but here is another one that takes the matter even further:

> (When you give) God is able to make it up to you by giving you everything you need and more, so that there will not only be enough for your need, but plenty left over to give joyfully to others.
>
> 2 Corinthians 9:8, The Living Bible

The Scripture is clear: The more generous you are, the more generous your heavenly Father will be. As in all of our actions as Christians, it's our *motive* that God is interested in. To give generously in order to be blessed does not seem to be a proper motive. Giving out of a sense of failure or guilt, trying to buy God's favor, is not responsible stewardship. Instead, I believe giving on faith is done in the life of a Christian as he hears in his heart the voice of God, discerns with his spirit the nudge of the Holy Spirit, and then obeys that call or that nudge.

An emotion-packed appeal for help comes in the mail. The pastor announces a special collection. A Christian radio station pleads for necessary funds to stay on the air. As such requests reach a Christian, he or she needs only to be quiet for a moment before the Lord to hear His yes or no. If the answer is yes, often the amount to give is impressed on the hearer's heart. Or there are times when I believe the asking Christian will hear the words, "No, I am not calling you to help here at this time." This listening is important to keep our motives for giving pure.

The important thing to remember in this matter of giving in faith is to be obedient to the nudge that God gives. Sometimes the gift He wants you to give will be small in comparison to other gifts; other times it will seem overly generous. It's not the size of your gift but loving obedience to the inner voice of God that brings God's blessing.

Pat tells the story of a moment of obedience in her life when the gift she was asked to give didn't amount to more than a few pennies. The story takes place back in the early days of our marriage when money was scarce and the pleasure of something really special to eat was rare. One afternoon at the grocery store we decided the time had come to treat ourselves. For forty-six cents we bought a package of frozen, breaded prawns. That night when our two young sons were tucked in bed, we went out to the kitchen, carefully deep fried the prawns and divided them between us. Altogether there were seventeen. Pat dished them out, eight for herself, nine for me. They lay on our plates, crispy and golden with an aroma that only those who have been truly hungry can appreciate.

We sat across from each other and tried to make conversation so that the treat would last as long as possible. I don't know if Pat talked more than me or if I ate faster than she did. All too soon I had none left, Pat had two. She claims that one of the most generous things she's ever done was to obey the nudge of the Holy Spirit and reach across the table to put one of her prawns on my plate. I ate it, not realizing the cost.

Throughout the years prawns remained a favorite of ours and especially of Pat's. It seemed there was never enough when we had them. Then, almost before we knew it, both the boys we had tucked in bed that night were teenagers and were working in adjacent fish-and-chip bars. Night after night one or the other would bring home leftover prawns to their mother until prawns became as commonplace as popcorn for an evening snack. When at last Pat had had her fill, that was the end of the leftovers that came home.

Pat's motive for giving me that one prawn had nothing to do with repayment, yet her gift was returned in just the way the Scriptures promised: full measure, pressed down and running over.

Warren Brenning tells of the time when he was in Sweden with his family preparing to go behind the Iron Curtain. Through a series of misadventures the thousand dollars with which he had left home had run out. All he had left was forty dollars which he needed for the ferry trip to Finland. Then Warren found himself in the same auditorium with Brother Andrew, the famous smuggler of Bibles to those who live under Communist dominion. As Warren heard Brother Andrew speak, his heart was greatly touched. Reaching into his wallet he joyfully gave him all he had.

Two days went by. It was almost time to take the ferry on the next lap of the family's journey. Even though Warren had no regrets over giving away their ferry fare, he was growing tense. The family's provisions had almost run out. Quite by chance the dean of the Storkyrken, the church which the King of Sweden attended, happened to hear the Brenning family sing. He invited them to the famous church to sing for the All Saint's Day liturgy. After finishing up the last few crackers, jelly, and cheese that were on hand, the family sang their hearts out for the people of the church. At the close the dean placed an envelope in Warren's hands. The family eagerly stopped under the first street light they came to, to see what it held. Warren opened the envelope and out fell a sheaf of Swedish kronor. There were 250, enough to feed the hungry family that night, pay for the ferry trip, eat again, buy the gas they needed — even after giving a tithe! The unexpected gift amounted to much more than what Warren had given to Brother Andrew.

Marilyn Bair tells of a story of obedience and the nudge of the Holy Spirit. It happened during a time when, as usual, their finances seemed precarious. Among other things, they had hoped to be able to buy the house they lived in for the Bair Foundation but the down payment was too high for a man without a stable income.

During the first week of December Marilyn received a $100 check from the Christmas Club. It was welcome beyond words; it was her only source of money for all her Christmas shopping. She spoke to the Lord, "Jesus, I'm going to give 10 percent of the money to World Vision to help the world's hungry children."

The Lord replied, "Marilyn, give it all."

"But, Lord, this money is not for me, it's for the family."

The answer came back, tender but insistent, "I want it all."

"Well, Lord, let me discuss it with the children."

That night Marilyn told Bill, their girls and the current foster children what she was sure the Lord had said.

"What shall I do?" she asked them.

"Mom," Jeanne answered, "if you think the Lord said give it, then give it."

"But it's the money for your Christmas gifts."

"Go ahead, Mom." It was a unanimous agreement.

Marilyn mailed the check. As Christmas grew close she began expecting some kind of reimbursement. None came; no money from the fraternity houses, no gifts from the clothing store, nothing. "It's O.K., Lord," Marilyn spoke to Him, "when I gave I didn't expect You to give in return. It's just that, well, I know You're generous and that $100 is nothing for You."

Two days before Christmas, Bill Bair answered the phone, listened for a few minutes and then shouted loud enough for the whole family to hear, "Praise the Lord!" The family came running and with one hand over the receiver Bill explained the call was from a man representing a group of businessmen who would like to buy the home they lived in and give it to them for a Christmas present. The next day they would send a check for $20,000 to arrange the down payment. The men had pledged themselves to pay the balance of $47,000 in the next two years.

True, there were no splashy personal gifts that year, but the gift of firsthand knowledge of God's generosity in their lives was a greater gift by far. It was given, Marilyn firmly believes, because the family was obedient in giving first.

In this chapter we've only mentioned a few ways that a Christian can live more closely to God in the area of finances. If the Lord has called you at this particular time to look to Him for your daily bread then it's because He wants to provide it for you and in doing so lead you to a life of deeper trust in Him.

If you are nudged by the Holy Spirit to give, then do so without guilt or secret desire to get something in return. When God gives back in full measure, pressed down, overflowing, receive what He gives you spiritually as well as materially.

12
Your Personal Financial Plan

YOU ARE NOW READY TO GO AHEAD and work out your own financial plan. Following this chapter are four blank schedules that you can use. They will give you a good understanding of your financial position as you fill them in. Before long you will be able to develop a plan patterned to your own specific needs.

Remember that you and your family are uniquely created by God. You have God-given gifts and talents which will show themselves in your financial plan. If your gift is hospitality you will probably spend more for food, decorating and other things relating to entertaining than someone whose gift is administration. The gift of creativity may mean a husband will want to fix up an older house, or a wife will be able to sew or paper and paint, and save paying for these things.

Every family also has priorities concerning what money should be spent on. Some people feel that a vacation spent in motels with swimming pools and eating in restaurants is absolutely necessary. Others feel that taking a tent to the woods is the way to go.

I remember now with some humor the first financial plan I worked up for someone else at their request. I planned a budget for them based on their newly lowered income. In my ignorance I used my own priorities. Since Pat and I were at a point where we had to cut every possible corner with food and clothing purchases, I presumed everyone else was willing to get by in the same way.

Later I found out they were aghast at the small amount I allowed them for food and clothing. I had made them feel so guilty every time they overspent, that for years after they apologized whenever they wore something new or were "caught" at a supermarket with luxuries in their basket. Needless to say, my personal budget didn't work for them.

The whole episode taught me clearly how priorities differ from one family to another. In making your financial plan, if you feel fifty dollars a week is the right amount for you to spend weekly on food, then do not be concerned about your neighbor's budget. He may think you are a spendthrift in one area while you are tempted to believe him a spendthrift in another. Actually, you have different lifestyles.

These limitations and different priorities are the basis for many disagreements between married couples. If both husband and wife recognize the unique personalities of their spouses, the financial limitations of the family, what financial commitments have been made with their money, and how much is available to spend on other things, they are well on their way to a successful financial management plan.

You may want to refer to Jim and Debby's schedules in chapter 3 as you prepare your own financial plan.

Schedule One — Summary of Income and Expenditures

The top section has spaces for you to list all your sources of income, how often you receive it (period: weekly, monthly or annually), the amount you expect to receive, and a place for some comments. The first entry would probably be for your salary. You should write in the estimated *net amount* (take-home pay) and not the gross amount. If you have a *weekly* pay check period, every third month you will receive five pay checks instead of four and the amount of this fifth check should be shown. If you anticipate a tax refund or an annual dividend during the six month budget period it should also be shown. Items such as babysitting income or sewing income, money from reserve or national guard duty should also be included.

The bottom section is for you to list all the expenses you expect to have in the next six months such as rent or house payment, medical insurance, phone, etc. The *total balance column* is used to show the total amount owed on each item, no matter how long it will take to pay it off. For instance if you are buying a car and still owe ten monthly payments of $100 each, the total balance you will write down is $1000 — the result of multiplying 10 times 100.

The *period payments column* is the place to write amount

paid every week, month, or quarter. The small space under period payments is used to identify how often the payment is made. You can use the following identifiers to indicate the periods:

w — weekly
m — monthly
q — quarterly
sa — semi-annually
a — annually

Other identifiers may be used for semi-monthly or other time periods.

Some of the payments will be the same every month and the periodic payment can be easily determined. Others, such as food, clothing and repairs may vary from month to month. It may be necessary to keep track of these items for a short period of time before you are able to estimate how much is spent on them. The longer you maintain a financial plan the more accurately you will be able to estimate them.

The first schedule of yours should include all sources of income (after taxes and other deductions) and all items of expenditures. After completing it, double check your schedule to insure every anticipated item is included.

Schedule Two — Six-month Cash Projection.

This schedule is based on the information shown on Schedule One. The first step is to write the next six months in the column headings. For instance if you are preparing your plan in May the months of June through November should be used for your plan.

A projection of income and expense items by *month* is prepared to get an idea of where you are headed. All entries should reflect cash transactions. For instance, the amount of income from your job should be the net amount you receive after all deductions have been made. If you get paid weekly, every third month you will get an extra check, but you will also have an extra week's expenses that month. Both of these items should be taken into consideration. Any dividends, bonuses, or one-time cash receipts such as income tax refunds should be considered on the projection. The *beginning balance* of the first month is the amount of money you have on hand in the bank at the start of the first month.

The expenditures should include an estimate of all monthly payments including periodic payments such as annual or semi-annual insurance policies. Other items that are paid quarterly such as water or garbage bills should also be shown *in the month that payment will be made.* An estimate for food, clothing, car expenses, entertainment, and "other" should be made. This is also the time to plan for Christmas or vacation time, depending on what time of the year it is when the projection is being prepared.

A six-month period is generally the right length for a family budget. It is long enough to determine where you are going and yet enable you to make changes in your spending, if required. It is current enough for you to have definite ideas and plans on what is to be done. There is nothing wrong with an annual budget or even a five-year look ahead, particularly for planning major decisions such as a move or change in jobs. For day to day planning, however, six months is a workable span of time.

After you have estimated what your cash income and expenditures for each of the next six months will be, the following steps should be taken.

1. Add your beginning balance to the income items in the first month's column to arrive at the total income for that month.

2. Add the expenditure items in the first month's column to arrive at the total expenditures for that month.

3. Subtract your total expenditures from your total income to arrive at an *ending balance.* This answer will be a minus (or negative) amount if your expenditures are greater than your income.

4. Add the income items for each of the following months to arrive at a total income amount for each month.

5. Add the expenditure items for each of the following months to arrive at a total expenditure amount for each month.

6. Subtract each total expenditures from the corresponding total income to arrive at the ending balance for each month.

7. There may be some months where money is left over and

98

other months where there is not enough money. In order to determine how much you will have to reduce expenditures or how much extra money you will have in the period a cumulative ending balance is required. To obtain the cumulative balance for the second month add the ending balance of the first two months together. To get a six month cumulative balance add all six month's ending balances.

Schedule Three — Recommendations

After completing the first two schedules, the time has come to analyze your financial situation and put down some recommendations or revisions on Schedule Three. Every item on Schedule Two should be looked at carefully to see if or how it can be changed. This is a time when prayer can be of great value. Ask the Lord to give you wisdom and willingness as you think of ways to reduce your expenses. Some questions you might want to ask are:

Did I include *every* source of income?
Did I calculate my estimated future salary correctly?
Should I consider a different job?
Should I consider part-time work?
Is there anything, such as a hobby, that I am doing that could be converted into income?

When looking at your expense items you should consider such questions as:

Is this item necessary?
Can I get along without it?
Should I reduce it? (or increase it?)
If so, how?
If I reduce it, will it cause increases in other expenses?
What changes will it make in my lifestyle to increase or decrease this item?
What are the alternatives?
What is its impact or relative importance to the total budget?

Every item including house payments or rent, car payments, and contributions should be looked at. You may discover that some items should be increased while others are way too high and need to be decreased. A guiding factor to your decision is the ending balance. If your projection shows you spending more money than you're making, it is obvious you must either increase your income or reduce your spending or both. *How* and *where* you do that should be recorded on the Recommendations Schedule.

Some specific recommendations might include the following:

1. *Reduce rent by moving to a different apartment.*

   When considering a move, the six-month savings should be compared to the cost of moving to see what the net savings would be.

2. *Reduce utilities.*

   Keep the thermostat lower, particularly at night. Cut down the number and length of long distance phone calls. Don't leave lights on when no one is in the room. Only run the dishwasher and washing machine when they are full. Fix leaky faucets.

3. *Sell a second car.*

   While this will cause considerable inconvenience, it will also result in a considerable saving. The gasoline and oil costs plus required insurance and maintenance over a six month period is a substantial sum of money. If the car is being bought on time this would also eliminate one of your larger monthly payments.

4. *Re-assess club and organization memberships.*

5. *Eliminate the use of charge accounts.*

   While this sounds like a simple method it is very hard to put into practice. There is a time when it will seem as if you are increasing expenses; you are paying the credit installments plus new cash purchases. This transition

100

period is difficult but two things should be remembered. First, the credit accounts will eventually be paid up. Second, when they are paid up you will have much more flexibility with your budget.

6. *Get by on present clothing.*

7. *Re-evaluate insurance payments.*

Very few people have excessive insurance coverage and it seldom pays to cancel or consolidate policies into new ones.

8. *Decide now how much to spend on vacations and Christmas.*

These two times should be among the most joyful and happy of any time in the year, yet for many families they are not. There are usually many reasons for tension besides financial ones, but the lack of proper financial planning can be the cause of unhappiness and conflicts within the family.

A vacation could be a long expensive trip or a short one or two-day outing. Gift giving at Christmas is often overdone, abused, and turns this holy day into a secular holiday. If celebrated in moderation it can add to the peace and joy of the season.

Planning for these two events can be done monthly by setting a sum of money aside or using special money such as income tax refunds, dividends, or a bonus for them. Whatever the source, you should know how much you can spend and not exceed that amount.

Schedule Four — Six-month Cash Budget

When you have completed the review of every item on Schedule Two and determined how you will reduce costs (if necessary) and what other revisions you will make, it is time to prepare the Six-month Cash Budget. This schedule is based on the information contained in the first three schedules.

The first step is to put the names of the next six months in the column headings. The budget section of this schedule will be the items on Schedule Two — Six Month Cash Projection adjusted by Schedule Three — Recommendations. For instance, on Jim and Debby's Schedule Two — Six Month Cash Projection, they estimated heat would cost $30 a month On Schedule Three — Recommendation, they decided to reduce the thermostat and save $8 per month. The difference, $22, was the amount they entered on Schedule Four — Six Month Cash Budget.

When all your income and adjusted expenditure items have been entered in the budget column, calculate the first month's ending balance by subtracting your total expenditures from your total income. This amount should then be entered as the beginning balance for the second month. When the second (and each succeeding) month's income is determined, the beginning balance should be added to the other income items.

The cash budget has an additional column for each month that is to be used to record your *actual expenses*. The main reason for this schedule is to guide you and help you follow the budget. It also gives you a check list to insure all your bills get paid.

At the end of each month when your actual income and expenditures are entered on Schedule Four — Six Month Cash Budget, you may want to update the next month's budget to reflect differences between last month's "actual" and "budget."

If a look at your six-month projection shows that even in six months with no charging at all your charge accounts won't be paid up, then you know it will be another six months and maybe more, before you can make any charge purchases. Some counselors say that the average American family can be debt-free if they do not charge anything for fourteen months. Don't be discouraged if it takes even longer.

As you make a commitment not to charge anything until all your charge accounts are paid off, I suggest that you make it a matter of prayer. Whether you pray together as husband and wife, outloud or silently, or whether one person does it alone, write it down on paper that you have promised not to charge until your account is paid off. Then tuck that piece of paper into a place where you will run across it from time to time. As you pray, ask for more strength than you've ever had before because not charging is very difficult for most American adults.

During this time of commitment, the worst part is the first few months. From that point on many people say that not charging until their accounts are paid off becomes almost a point of honor. They can see they are going to get out of their financial mess and the interim agony is worth it.

If this is your time not to charge anything until your credit balances are zero then the excitement is just beginning, for trusting God is an adventure. With what appears to be planned obsolescence, you can presume before your debts are paid off that you will need some kind of new appliance. You can be sure that the children will need warm coats and that either husband or wife will need some clothes. Since you made a commitment not to charge, what do you do? This is where being a Christian makes all the difference in the world. For maybe the first time in your life you will begin to know what it means to live by faith.

It will mean trusting God to send extra money for your real needs or to send a stove or coat or pair of shoes. It will mean being patient and trusting Him when everything seems impossible. But God does do the impossible for those who will sincerely ask and believe that He will do it. When you have walked this way with the Lord in new trust, you'll find your spiritual life will reach a level you once envied in others but never thought possible for yourself.

Before you know it the time will come when you are debt-free and able to make credit purchases again. At this wonderful point in your life, do not let a department store credit department make the choice of how much you can spend. You have worked too long and hard to get out of debt to throw it all away.

Look at your financial plan. See how much you have been spending on time payments. It is reasonable to say that you can either pay cash for, or charge, *two-thirds of that amount.* If you had been spending one hundred dollars a month in payments, you can now allow yourself sixty-seven dollars for household and clothing expenses. The remaining thirty-three dollars gives you a surplus to work with at the end of each month.

If you remember, I asked Jim and Debby to list their needs

and wants in separate columns. This is an important step for anyone who wants spending guidelines. Debby's and Jim's list of needs were surprising to me as they were different from my own. Both of them felt dining out to be a want not a need, while Pat and I decided long ago that time together over a meal someone else cooked was something we both needed. Your lists of needs and wants will be different than mine or anyone else's. Once you've made your lists, confine your spending to those things that are needs only. The wants should only be provided for out of your surplus.

If you choose to start charging again, now is the time for your charge-plate to bring you God's blessing in a new way. The old temptations to purchase this one lovely thing for the children, or to buy the coat you've always dreamed of having, will all come back. You know that stores encourage you to go ahead and buy. Satan will tell you that you owe it to yourself to have it. The temptation is to give in to pride and greed.

What will you do? What kind of a choice will you make? It's at this point that you call on Jesus for help. Alone you can't do battle, but with Him you will be able. Just as Jim talked over that chain saw with the Lord, so you can speak to Jesus as you would to any friend. "Lord, You know I don't have to have this. You know it would be wrong since no matter how I try to convince myself, I can't pay for it when the bill is due. Lord, strengthen me to choose correctly, to lay it down (or hang it back up) and walk out of this department."

If you pray this way, Jesus will answer your call immediately. What's more the Bible is full of promises to those who say no to temptation. You will become special to the Lord (Deut. 4:30-31), all will go well with you (Deut. 5:29), your days will be long (1 Kings 3:14), your deeds shall be blessed (James 1:25). These are only samples of the things God has in store for you — gifts that money cannot buy.

In the first chapter we learned that Achan and his family lost everything because he chose to give in to greed. Jim and Debby almost lost their marriage and possessions, almost gave up the security of a happy home for their children because they couldn't stop buying. Maybe only you know how close you have come to being like Achan or Jim and Debby.

Choose today a new way. Choose to make out your personal plan. Choose not to charge until you are out of debt. Choose to limit yourself to needs. Just as Joseph chose God's way and blessing came to him beyond his fondest dreams, so it is today with many who have stuck to their financial plans. So it can be with you.

Appendix

Reconciling Your Bank Statement

It's not unusual to have trouble reconciling your checkbook and bank statement. Often the reason for this is that you forget to enter every check and every deposit. Another is that you have not been careful to enter exactly the right amounts. Or that you use your checkbook for memos, reminders, grocery lists, etc. Checks should be entered by number, date, and amount. A running balance after each entry (deposit or check written) should be kept, so you know your bank balance at all times.

When your bank statement arrives, open it and reconcile it with your bankbook within two or three days after receiving it. All cancelled checks received from the bank should be sorted *by number,* and marked (✓) in your checkbook.

Step #1
Write the final balance shown on the bank statement in the upper right hand part of a piece of paper. The left side of the paper may be used as a worksheet.

Balance (bank) $396.12

Step # 2
Total up any deposits that are recorded in your checkbook but are not shown on the bank statement. Add this total to the figure used in step # 1. If there are none, forget this step.

Balance (bank)	$396.12
Deposits not shown by bank	(+) 15.00
	411.12

Step # 3
Find the total of your outstanding checks (those entries in your checkbook you could not mark off because the checks had not been returned to you).

Step #4
Subtract this total (step #3) from the addition done in step #2. (Or, if this step was skipped, from the balance shown by the bank.)

Balance (bank)	$396.12
Deposits now shown by bank	(+) 15.00
	411.12
Outstanding checks	(—) 28.56
	$382.56

Step #5
Draw a line all the way across your piece of paper. Write the final balance shown in your checkbook just below the line, and *add* any deposits that are shown on the bank statement but not in your checkbook. (Because you forgot!) Take time to add them to your checkbook now.

Balance (checkbook)	$319.33
Deposits (not recorded in checkbook)	(+) 65.23
	384.56

Step # 6

Subtract any bank service charges, charges for new checks, etc., as shown on your statement, and subtract them in your checkbook, too.

Balance (checkbook)	$319.33
Deposits (not recorded in checkbook)	(+) 65.23
	384.56
Service charges	(—) 2.00
	$382.56

The two final figures (one on the upper part of the page, and one on the lower part), should be identical.

If the two final figures do not agree:

(a) look to see if all outstanding checks were listed
(b) make sure all checks written were listed in your checkbook
(c) compare the amount of each check with the amount shown on the bank statement
(d) compare deposits made with the amount shown
(e) check the arithmetic in your checkbook

If you are still not able to reconcile your statement, take your checkbook, cancelled checks, and bank statement to the bank and ask them to help. Don't keep carrying an error from month to month in your checkbook.

Additional sets of the four financial schedules are available from Women's Aglow Fellowship, P.O. Box I, Dept. MT, Lynnwood, WA 98036, at a cost of fifty cents each set.